# Retirementology®

| DATE DUE | |
|----------|--|
| | |
| | |
| | |
| | |
| | |
| | |
| | |
| | |
| | |
| | |
| | |
| | |
| | |
| | |
| | |
| | |
| | |

DEMCO, INC. 38-2931

# Retirementology®

## Rethinking the American Dream in a New Economy

Gregory Salsbury, Ph.D.

Vice President, Publisher: Tim Moore
Associate Publisher and Director of Marketing: Amy Neidlinger
Executive Editor: Jim Boyd
Editorial Assistant: Pamela Boland
Development Editor: Russ Hall
Operations Manager: Gina Kanouse
Senior Marketing Manager: Julie Phifer
Publicity Manager: Laura Czaja
Assistant Marketing Manager: Megan Colvin
Cover Designer: Anne Jones
Managing Editor: Kristy Hart
Senior Project Editor: Lori Lyons
Copy Editor: Apostrophe Editing Services
Proofreader: Kay Hoskin
Indexer: Erika Millen
Compositor: Nonie Ratcliff
Manufacturing Buyer: Dan Uhrig

© 2010 by Pearson Education, Inc.
Publishing as FT Press
Upper Saddle River, New Jersey 07458

**This book is sold with the understanding that neither the author nor the publisher is engaged in rendering legal, accounting, estate planning, tax, or other professional services or advice by publishing this book. Each individual situation is unique. Thus, if legal or financial advice or other expert assistance is required in a specific situation, the services of a competent professional should be sought to ensure that the situation has been evaluated carefully and appropriately. The author and the publisher disclaim any liability, loss, or risk resulting directly or indirectly, from the use or application of any of the contents of this book.**

FT Press offers excellent discounts on this book when ordered in quantity for bulk purchases or special sales. For more information, please contact U.S. Corporate and Government Sales, 1-800-382-3419, corpsales@pearsontechgroup.com. For sales outside the U.S., please contact International Sales at international@pearson.com.

Company and product names mentioned herein are the trademarks or registered trademarks of their respective owners and are not sponsoring, endorsing, promoting, or selling specific financial products or endorsing any opinions expressed herein.

Printed in the United States of America
Third Printing June 2010

Paperback:
ISBN-10: 0-13-705653-2
ISBN-13: 978-0-13-705653-8

Hardcover:
ISBN-10: 0-13-217226-7
ISBN-13: 978-0-13-217226-4

Pearson Education LTD.
Pearson Education Australia PTY, Limited.
Pearson Education Singapore, Pte. Ltd.
Pearson Education North Asia, Ltd.
Pearson Education Canada, Ltd.
Pearson Educación de Mexico, S.A. de C.V.
Pearson Education—Japan
Pearson Education Malaysia, Pte. Ltd.

*Library of Congress Cataloging-in-Publication Data*
Salsbury, Gregory B. (Gregory Brandon)
  Retirementology : rethinking the American dream in a new economy / Gregory Salsbury.
     p. cm.
  Includes bibliographical references and index.
  ISBN-13: 978-0-13-705653-8 (pbk. : alk. paper)
  ISBN-10: 0-13-705653-2 (pbk. : alk. paper) 1. Retirement—United States—Planning.
2. Retirement—Economic aspects—United States. 3. Baby boom generation—
United States. I. Title.
  HQ1063.2.U6S25 2010
  306.3'80973—dc22
                              2009051045

Dedicated to my mother Inge Salsbury,
a survivor of America's Great Depression—
with hopes that the lessons of her era
will help us with the current mess.

A special thank you to Phil Wright and his team,
who stuck with this project over a couple of years
of research, interviews, and debates, along
with late night and early morning calls and
email—and the usual last-minute edits.

# Contents

# Acknowledgments

I would like to extend my thanks and appreciation to the following people who have contributed to the creative and technical development of this project: C. Philip Wright, Tamu McCreary, Larissa Agazzi, DeAnna Hemmings, Scott Forbes, Scott Rolsen, Douglas Mantelli, John Koehler, Jeremy Rafferty, Tom Hurley, Andy Silver, Ryan Riggen, Nathan Timmons, Dan Starishevsky, Kathy Schofield, Diane Montana, Jeff Bain, Mary Walensa, Jeff Thompson, Eiden Herring, Peter Muckley, Kelly Eden, Kenneth Smith, Steve Luckenbach, Jim Boyd, Lori Lyons, Eric Palumbo, and Danny Rubin (cover art).

# About the Author

**Gregory Salsbury, Ph.D.** is Executive Vice President of Jackson National Life Distributors LLC (JNLD) and a much sought-after industry speaker on the subjects of investor behavior, adviser best practices, and retirement.

Salsbury received a master's degree in communications from the University of Illinois, and a second master's degree in communication technologies from the Annenberg School of Communications. He received his doctorate in organizational communication from the University of Southern California and is published in the areas of sales, marketing, employee motivation, behavioral finance, and retirement. From his work and experience as a long-standing executive in the financial services industry, Salsbury was uniquely positioned to craft a visionary view of retirement's future. His landmark book, *But What If I Live? The American Retirement Crisis®*, was a wake-up call for a generation of undersaved, overspent, and unprepared Baby Boomers.

# Preface

I had what I thought was a great idea for a new book—a blend of two equally powerful and timely topics. The first topic deals with America's retirement crisis and the challenge of prudent retirement planning in the midst of it. This subject provided the foundation for my first book, *But What If I Live? The American Retirement Crisis.* The topic remains of massive importance right now as the 77 million members of America's most celebrated demographic group—the Baby Boomers—are commencing retirement.[1] For the most part, the same behavior that created the challenges in the first place is continuing or accelerating. This painful conclusion led me to the second topic.

There is a relatively new field of work developing around psychology and finance, known alternatively as behavioral economics or behavioral finance. It focuses on how investor psychology—attitudes, biases, and emotions—impacts financial decisions and behavior. Behavioral finance researchers ask questions like: *Why will people drive 45 minutes to use a $2.00 coupon? Why will people wash their own car on a Saturday morning to save 10 bucks, but would scoff at the idea of washing their neighbor's car for $10? Why won't people sell a poor performing stock just because they inherited it from grandma? Why do people spend differently with a credit card than they do with cash? Why do millions of people believe that they paid no income taxes because they received a refund?* The painfully clear message from behavioral finance research is this: When it comes to money, people don't always behave rationally.

I thought that the application of behavioral finance to retirement planning would be an engaging project—as much fun for me to explore as, hopefully, it would be to read. But a funny thing happened to my storyline along the way. In 2008, the market and economy crashed with a ferocity not seen in decades, and I suddenly had a third act to this play.

As the Meltdown of 2008 was unfolding, I was the keynote speaker for an industry conference in Chicago. My subject—scheduled nearly a year in advance—was "The American Retirement Crisis." With tongue firmly implanted in cheek, I began by telling the audience that I had good news for them, and I put up my first slide, which read:

# The retirement crisis is over.

I then explained that this was because—and I clicked to my second slide, which read:

# Retirement is over.

It drew some nervous laughs, because people got the point: There was a retirement crisis before all financial hell broke loose, but now we have a *real* mess.

In fact, now we have investor psychology meeting retirement planning in the midst of a monumental financial meltdown. How has this new environment impacted some of the classic behavioral finance biases? And what should pre-retirees and retirees do about all this? These are the essential questions that *Retirementology* has identified. In the process, I hope to

- Identify the classic mistakes we are all making with our thinking and behavior in the key areas of earning, spending, saving, borrowing, and investing.
- Understand the scope of the financial meltdown and how it has amplified the impact of our mistakes.
- Connect those mistakes to the retirement planning process and discuss possible options to help readers aim for retirement.

*Retirementology* is not a typical retirement planning book, nor is it a book on psychology; it is a little bit of both. Part of what has created a retirement crisis in America is the tendency to treat retirement as a separate and static event, relegate it to a zone, or even compartmentalize it. In this regard, many seem to act as if retirement planning were divorced from other monetary behavior. Quite the contrary, retirement should be viewed as a process—one that begins as soon as you engage in earning, saving, spending, borrowing, or investing. Indeed, all these things are inextricably bound. For example, a pre-retirement couple may have a choice between buying a new $55,000 automobile or buying a $35,000 pre-owned automobile and putting the remaining $20,000 in a vehicle of a different sort—a retirement account. Such decisions may have a profound impact on their lifestyles in retirement. In this regard, you can't actually build a solid approach to retirement without also tackling your approach to all the other fiscal decisions in your life. That is why behavioral finance plays such a key role in retirement planning. If we truly want to plan correctly for retirement, we need to address the mistakes we have made, and may still be making, with regard to how we think about money, how we feel about money, and how we behave with money.

In developing this book, our research team conducted nearly a dozen focus group interviews with pre-retirees and retirees, ranging in ages from 25 to 70. Our researchers posed a number of questions on topics such as the housing crisis, family issues, overspending, investor behavior, and more. Some of the responses are included in relevant chapters throughout the book and specifically identified as findings from our focus group research. In other cases, hypothetical names, people, and situations have been used to illustrate points. For example, *Retirementology* introduces some one-of-a-kind terms, descriptions, and scenarios, which have been created to help you better understand a number of the behaviors associated with investor psychology.

In fact, the title of our book is a one-of-a-kind term...

---

**RETIREMENTOLOGY:** [ri-*tahy*ᵘʰ r-muhnt-*ol*-uh-jee]

A new way of thinking about retirement planning that considers both psychology and finance against a backdrop of the worst economic crisis since the Great Depression.

---

# Introduction

**RETIREWENT:** [ri-*tahy*<sup>uh</sup> r-went]

What happened to the retirement hopes and dreams of Americans after the meltdown. *Roger and Dee both had to take on second jobs thanks to retirewent.*

## Paradigm Lost

The greatest bull market in history was a glorious thing. When the bull finally keeled over from exhaustion at the end of 1999, it ended a 20-year period in which the S&P 500® Index saw an annual average return of 18.5%.[1] Encompassed within that period were 5 consecutive years of 20% plus returns.[2] The impact of that 5-year period on the psyches, not just the portfolios, of investors shouldn't be underestimated.

Picture Herb, a hypothetical ultraconservative investor, who years or decades earlier had sworn off of equity investments, which are a stock or security in which an investor can buy ownership and which involve financial risk, including loss of principal. Since 1982, Herb's brother-in-law has been telling him that he's missing the boat. *"Herb, I've shaved 15 years off of my retirement date. I'll be on the beach about 5 years from now. You are too conservative, Herb."* Well, Herb smiled politely and ignored such comments for the first few years, and said to himself, *"Slow and steady wins the race. This growth and tech stuff is just a fad. This can't continue."* But it did continue, not just for a few months or years, but for more than a decade—and then it accelerated. You could see it in the headlines of the day, as things like price-to-earnings ratio and profits became quaint notions from a former era.

"A Bull Market with Strong Legs and a Long Way to Go," *The New York Times*, May 7, 1995

"Economists Expect Little Trouble in Paradise," *Business Week*, December 30, 1996

"A new paradigm for the U.S. economy," *Chicago Fed Letter*, October 1998

"Investing: Is the P/E Ratio Becoming Irrelevant?" *The New York Times*, July 21, 2002

Gallup polls showed that investors ended the decade of the '90s with expectations of 19% annual returns on their investments, and they were expecting those returns to continue for another 10 years.[3] So when Herb saw his brother-in-law at Thanksgiving dinner in 1997, he had to listen to how much his brother-in-law's retirement portfolio had grown in the last 5 years. No sir; this wasn't even stock picking and hot tip stuff. *"Just believe in equities baby,"* Herb's brother-in-law proclaimed. After all, just consider how strongly the Dow Jones Industrial Average, an index which is a price-weighted average of 30 actively traded blue-chip stocks that are generally the leaders in their industry, performed during the 1990s[4]:

- Dow in Dec. 31, 1990—2,633.66
- Dow in Dec. 31, 1991—3,168.83
- Dow in Dec. 31, 1992—3,301.11
- Dow in Dec. 31, 1993—3,754.09
- Dow in Dec. 31, 1994—3,834.44
- Dow in Dec. 31, 1995—5,117.12
- Dow in Dec. 31, 1996—6,448.27
- Dow in Dec. 31, 1997—7,908.25
- Dow in Dec. 31, 1998—9,181.43, *up 249% from Dec. 31, 1990*
- Dow in Dec. 31, 1999—11,497.12, *up 337% from Dec. 31, 1990*

*The Dow Jones Industrial Average is an unmanaged index and not available for direct investment.*

And finally, Herb just couldn't take it anymore. Enough was enough. He could do better, he thought. So he made the bold decision to dip his toe in the water. He took 20% of his $250,000 retirement portfolio and put it in equities. To his delight, Herb watched that 20% grow by 28% that year—$50,000 from his portfolio became $64,000. He then shifted another 25% of his portfolio, putting $50,000 into equities, and watched it grow by 21% the next year, as $114,000 became $138,000. He was up $38,000 in his portfolio in just 2 years. It took 17 years, but he was now a convert.

So how does this sad, and possibly familiar, story end? The beach was more than in sight for Herb. He could taste the salt air. Then came the Meltdown of 2008, and it was like a small tsunami hit his beach. And a generation of Baby Boomers suffered a total loss of $4 trillion in retirement accounts, or roughly 40% of America's GDP, with rising debt and a declining stock market representing the worst post-war downturn for *household wealth* since the recession of 1973–75.[5] The *Herbs* of the world were hurt pretty badly—especially if they were on the doorstep of retirement. Some of them swore they would never invest in the market again—and haven't. But most others, even though a bit shell-shocked and hurt, held out hope of a quick recovery. It just seemed more reasonable that the previous years were the benchmark for normalcy—not the Meltdown of 2008.

Yes sir; the new paradigm was intact, it just had a bit of a hiccup along the way. The bursting of the tech bubble hit many portfolios hard, but at the time, left the rest of the economy fairly unscathed. But then the Meltdown of 2008...Boom! Like a speeding car running head on into a bridge abutment, the damage of this economic downturn went beyond the largest stock market downturn since the Great Depression. Housing, unemployment, escalating taxes, and inflation are all contributing to the situation. We are experiencing dramatic losses in wealth, performance, and investor faith. The shock waves are showing up in many and varied ways.

- Since 2004, the average Baby Boomer has seen his net worth decline by 45%.[6]
- Seven million jobs have been lost since the recession began in December 2007.[7]

- One-in-four mortgage owners in America is underwater[8] and one-in-nine housing units is vacant.[9]
- The Consumer Confidence Index has hit a record low[10] and consumer anxiety about interest rates and a lack of guaranteed income has more than doubled in the last three years.[11] In fact, 62% of American adults believe today's children will *not* be better off than their parents—up 15% since the beginning of 2009.[12]
- There were 35 corporate defaults in March 2009, the highest number of defaults in a single month since the Great Depression.[13]
- A quarter of U.S. employers have eliminated matching contributions to their 401(k) plans since September 2008.[14]

On the retail side, we saw record drops in sales—9.1% in the fourth quarter of 2008 from the previous year.[15] As a result, Best Buy shares fell 8% in November 2008 alone, and its stock has plummeted—down 58% in the first quarter of 2009. Best Buy Vice Chairman and CEO Brad Anderson cited *"rapid, seismic changes in consumer behavior"* and *"the most difficult climate we've ever seen"* as the causes.[16]

Said Brian Dunn, Best Buy president and COO, *"In 42 years of retailing, we've never seen such difficult times for the consumer."*[17] Starbucks, the unquestioned sultan of the minor indulgence, watched its earnings drop by 69% in the first quarter of 2009, and it has closed 900 stores since the summer of 2008.[18]

All of this has shaken confidence not just in investing, but also in the United States economy, the government, the global economy, and indeed, capitalism itself. A trifecta of tragedies in credit, capital, and liquidity has cut the world's economy to the core. Bad strategy and bad behavior in response have compounded the Meltdown of 2008. And it should be noted that the bad strategy has included some of what was touted as "best practice" retirement planning. No magic product exists today, and solving for retirement is and will likely remain a difficult and complex challenge. In Chapter 8, "Lost in Translation," I examine the difficulty of solving the retirement income riddle. It was already tough prior to the meltdown—now investors may need a translator to comprehend the new layers of complexity.

Further, that complexity is magnified when investor behavior, emotions, and biases come into play. And, as we will see, they come into play with nearly all the basic retirement planning questions: For how many years will you need retirement income? Emotions usually, and understandably, cloud the best attempts to soberly estimate that answer. What is a prudent annual rate of return to assume on your investments for a 20-, 30-, or 40-year period? As we have seen, investors a mere decade ago would have given a very different answer than those of today—an answer that likely varies by double digits. The same might be true for questions about assumed tax or inflation rates moving forward. All this will impact the question of how much you need to live on each year, hence how much you need to withdraw each year. Of course, how much you withdraw in retirement is irrelevant if you don't have the nest egg from which to withdraw in the first place. When it comes to building a nest egg, it is important to note that starting early is important.

A number of financial firms, however, have popularized the notion of a retirement zone, the few years remaining prior to entering retirement, as somehow the most critical to a successful retirement. In Chapter 3, "The NoZone," it becomes clear that solving the retirement conundrum requires attention much earlier than a handful of years prior to retirement...and will certainly continue well into retirement. According to the Employee Benefit Research Institute, when the financial crisis began, 25% of Americans between the ages of 55 and 65 had 90% or more of their money in stock funds of their 401(k)s, and undoubtedly have suffered greatly, losing nearly half of their account balances right on the eve of their retirement.[19] As a generation is forced to revisit and revise their retirement plans, they will truly understand the importance of compound interest and starting early. In fact, you might well argue that the handful of years in one's early twenties are the most critical years to retirement. Unfortunately, most future retirees at the dawn of their retirement planning journey are off to a slow start, as Hewitt and Associates reports that over 70% of Generation Y workers (those born in 1978 or later, now in the thick of their 20s) don't participate in employer-sponsored accounts.[20]

If savings is the yin, spending is the yang. In other words, while Americans haven't been saving, they have been spending, at least during the last 20 years.[21] In Chapter 2, "Gold Dust on Sushi," named after the Japanese practice that represented the height of 1980s overindulgence, we uncover the *carpe diem* spending mentality that resulted in a negative savings rate, high debt, and record bankruptcies. Household debt averages doubled from 2000–2007, totaling $13.8 trillion, or $46,115 per person.[22] America's savings rate had dipped into negative territory, which was the lowest since the Great Depression until people abruptly stopped spending as the market tumbled.[23] And bad behavior is magnifying these troubles; more than 20% of workers age 45 and up have stopped contributing to their 401(k)s.[24] In the course of developing the highest standard of living in the history of mankind, we have developed some bad habits. Chief among them is the American consumers' addiction to debt, which is closely related to our inability and unwillingness to manage money.

Further, some indulgences became so habitual and were so ingrained that they were no longer even seen as indulgences—and still may not be seen as such despite the economic meltdown. For example, although our friends at Starbucks have certainly seen a negative impact, many people see nothing extraordinary about handing over $7 at a time for a muffin and a coffee drink. It would be interesting to know the number of survivors of the Great Depression who have ever walked into a Starbucks and laid down several dollars for a drink. I'll go out on a limb and suggest the number is quite small. Similarly, many people have come to view a $50 to $100 per month bill for cable television or satellite coverage the same way that previous generations viewed a water bill. You don't think of not paying it; it's just one of life's necessities. Well, it may be time to hold the gold dust on that next order of sushi.

No place was the love affair with debt more out of control than with the nucleus of the American Dream—our homes. For tens of millions of Americans, those dreams have rapidly turned into nightmares. In Chapter 4, "House Money," you will see how many of the age-old axioms of home ownership are now being challenged. One deals with the core belief that a house is a solid long-term investment. We were taught that our homes might take modest dips in value here and there, but ultimately would always go up—even if that were over the course of a decade or two. Many Baby Boomers today, especially those in the most devastated metropolitan areas within Florida or in Las Vegas, as well as in cities such as Los Angeles, Phoenix, Ann Arbor, and Reno, are looking at home value declines that are so significant, they might not be recouped in their remaining lifetimes. And that stark fact is changing the way they view homes and home ownership in a host of interesting ways. How could home values have dropped so far so fast? Does it make sense to own any more?

In one of our focus groups, we heard from a mortgage lender who told us of a Boomer who had taken out a $100,000 equity loan on his house just to pay for his daughter's wedding because, as he stated, *"Seemed like a good idea at the time."* By his own definition, the man was *"never rich,"* but his house provided a fortress of overconfidence to overspend. When he came back in to see the lender after the meltdown, he was already underwater and was referred to the company's loan modification department. There are thousands of examples like this across the country, and after years of using their houses as personal ATMs, many Americans, like this gentleman, have seen their bedrock crack and crumble. In fact, many now see that their remaining retirement nest eggs are about equal to or even less than the amount of negative equity they have in their homes. There is one place where real estate is still hot. There is a booming market for the sale of burial plots by individuals, many of which have been in families for years, as record numbers of people are selling their final resting spots back to the cemetery and other buyers, often for a fraction of what they paid for them.[25]

What a difference a meltdown makes. I have been struck by the complete reversal in many investors' perspectives. Ask a Boomer today what he's thinking versus a year ago, and he's likely to tell you something like this, *"My wife and I just shake our heads...because less than a year ago, our biggest worries were about whether we should put granite or tile in the new bathroom; whether we should go back to Hawaii this year or venture to Italy; or whether we should put a lap pool in the backyard. Now those questions seem ridiculous compared to what we're wrestling with."*

This meltdown has not only hit our houses, it has invaded our homes and disrupted millions of American families. In the midst of recent economic and market turmoil, the evolution of family values is quickly becoming a revolution. In Chapter 5, aptly titled, "Family Matters," you'll see that today's family structure is at the core of emotional confusion and complexity in terms of spending, saving, investing, and retirement. My wife recently spent $30 on a T-shirt for our son. *"We're now buying $30 T-shirts for the kids?"* I objected. Clearly irritated, she explained to me that it was a great deal because it was high quality (from an upscale store), and it was on sale. I remember wearing jeans with patches sewn onto the knees—and this wasn't a fashion statement. As a kid, for my family to have spent a comparable amount on one of my T-shirts would have required that it double as my winter coat. I wouldn't even spend $30 on a T-shirt for myself today. But as many parents know, we will spend differently on our kids than on ourselves. (Now, for the record, after I told my wife that I would use this example in my book, she argued that it wasn't a T-shirt at all, but some sort of sport shirt. I saw it. It is green with no collar and short sleeves. It is a T-shirt.) Let's face it. The way we think, act, feel, behave, and interact within our family has a dramatic effect on long-term retirement planning.

Many American families are now hopeful that governmental response will be the answer to this economic crisis. There is no question that the response has been swift and unprecedented. If you add all the recent initiatives—The American Recovery and Reinvestment Act (the original "stimulus" package), the Troubled Asset Relief Program (TARP), and the spending and lending of the Fed, Treasury, and FDIC—the total is $9.7 trillion to stem the recession.[26] The impact on the record deficit is jaw dropping. We had a deficit issue before the new spending and bailouts. Our federal future obligations were already the equivalent of over $50 trillion, or a financial burden of $170,000 for every American.[27] This massive deficit begs the question of how it will be paid; and the obvious answer is that it will be necessary to raise taxes. Here's some of what the taxman is expected to bring with him.

- Tax increase of some $1.4 trillion over the next 10 years.[28]
- Increased taxes for 3.2 million taxpayers by an average of $300,000 over the next decade.[29]
- Allowing the 2001 and 2003 tax cuts to expire for couples making over $250,000 and singles earning over $200,000. This includes increases of rates on income, capital gains, and dividends.[30]
- Removal of key tax deductions.[31]
- Escalation in estate taxes.[32]
- New ways to disguise taxes by using other titles, such as fees, surcharges, penalties, and so on.[33]

In predicting the impact of all such changes, individual states are the proverbial canaries in the mineshaft. More than 10 states are considering or have implemented major increases to sales, corporate, or personal income taxes to fill their respective budget gaps.[34] Nationwide, we are seeing a physical, geographic bifurcation of givers and takers. Leading the way is California, the biggest canary, with a $45 billion shortfall,[35] massive debt that grows by $1.7 million every hour,[36] and a mass exodus of wealthy citizens fleeing for other states.[37] Now more than ever, controlling taxes will be one of the biggest challenges and one of the most important steps you will take toward retirement. Another obstacle standing between you and a comfortable retirement is healthcare. With costs rising at four times the rate of inflation,[38] it's no wonder 46 million Americans are now without health insurance.[39]

Let's face it. Healthcare in America is "Under the Knife," which is the title of Chapter 7 on this hot topic. As of this writing, a major national debate over healthcare and health insurance is taking place. The White House is pushing a plan that will essentially nationalize many healthcare functions, and proponents are insisting that the plan presently put forth will lower costs across the board while also covering more Americans, though not all Americans. To put Medicare in perspective, for example, consider the richest budget in U.S. history—$3.5 trillion—on top of the $787 billion "stimulus" package recently passed by Congress, and that is just a drop in the bucket compared to America's $32 trillion unfunded Medicare liability.[40] With retirement looming and government-sponsored healthcare programs in question, Americans face a greater reality that unplanned medical expenses may derail even the best-laid retirement plans.

# The "Ology" in Your So-Called Retirement

When it comes to *your* best-laid retirement plans, you can choose to be your own best friend or your own worst enemy. There is no shortage of responsibility for this financial mess. Take your pick: the Fed and its promotion of easy money; Congress and its turning a blind eye to pleas for lending review and reform; optimistic home buyers; greedy subprime lenders; out-of-touch appraisers; asleep-at-the-wheel ratings agencies; or Wall Street bankers. We can blame these folks all we like, but individual behavior played a large part in where many Americans are today. That's why behavioral finance is a key element of this book. It's a wonderfully controversial field, because it highlights how we behave in ways completely contrary to what logic or traditional economists might have predicted. Sound familiar?

How do people behave irrationally when it comes to money? Allow me to illustrate with a decision-making example. Imagine I have $1,000 to split between you and another person—I'll call that other person Samantha. The only stipulation is that Samantha gets to decide how the money is divided, and you must agree with that division. If you agree, you both leave with my $1,000. If you don't agree, I keep all my money. Let's assume that after careful consideration, Samantha decides that $980 of the $1,000 should go into her pocket, and that a mere $20 should go to you. Would you still agree with the deal? Now traditional economists will tell you to take the $20 and not be concerned with how much the other person keeps. They contend that people should try to spend as little as they can, save as much as they can, and get the maximum return on their investments for the smallest risk. In sum, people should act in a way that puts the most money in their own pockets. Per this view, the field of economics, and indeed retirement planning, is strictly a mathematical theory, and investors and markets are expected to behave in certain ways that are observable and predictable. In the field of economics, this is called the Expected Utility Theory.

During the exercise, I make certain to articulate that this is strictly "hypothetical" to protect myself from those rare instances when there is agreement between the two. But here's the catch: I can tell you that my $1,000 is rarely in jeopardy. The common responses are, *"No. I don't want the swine to get the money." "Absolutely not." "He can take his $20 and shove it."* You get the idea. I point out to these folks that up until I opened my little cash box, they had no expectation of receiving anything. And now some 120 seconds later, someone is trying to hand them a $20 bill, and they are spitting on it. No matter. This exercise is one of many examples of how people behave in ways that confound the traditional equity theorists. In fact, the quaint notion that people will behave in ways that are predictable and observable ignores what 2002 Nobel Prize winner in Economics Dr. Daniel Kahneman calls *"the human agent."* In an interview I conducted with Dr. Kahneman in 2004, this pioneer in behavioral finance told me about how his discipline doesn't assume perfect rationality, which is why perceptual bias, complexity, and emotions like pride and anger, illustrated in our exercise, can overshadow sound financial decisions.

For example, research from Dr. Kahneman and Dr. Amos Tversky showed that investors are more sensitive to decreases in the value of their portfolio than to increases in value.[41] Even in good times, many investors tend to suffer from what experts refer to as "myopic loss aversion"—a basic tenet from the field of behavioral finance, which holds that people psychologically weigh losses twice as heavily as gains.

Here's an example of myopic loss aversion.

I flip a coin:
Heads, you win $110.
Tails, you lose $100.
Will you take the bet?

Behavioral finance shows us that there will be few takers of the gamble. How much would most people need to win before they would

be willing to take the gamble? $120? $140? $180? The research reveals
before the majority of people will be willing to take the risk, they
would need to receive at least twice the amount of the possible loss.

> So the typical person won't take my gamble unless the gamble
> is improved.
>
> I flip a coin again and this time:
>
> Heads, you win $200.
>
> Tails, you lose $100.

Now that the upside is twice as good as the downside, more people will take me up on my second coin flip. Think of it this way—have
you lost $20 before? The regret attached to that loss is more powerful
than the joy you might feel if you found $40 on the sidewalk. (When I
was 14, someone stole $20 from my locker at a public swimming
pool—at a time when a typical two-hour lawn mowing job earned me
a whopping $4. You can tell that it stuck with me.) Ever lost your wal-
let or car keys...or at least thought you did? Your search in this scenario is all consuming, and the impending sense of loss overpowers all
other priorities.

Psychologists believe the human mind has two systems for decision making: intuitive and reasoning. Although experts would argue
that this division is often overly simplified, in general, the intuitive
system, located on the right side of the brain, is emotional and fast to
act but slow to learn. However, the reasoning system, located on the
left side of the brain, is more controlled, less emotional, focused on
rules, and slower to act. Neither side is always correct, but the intuitive side does have its flaws.

Dr. Kahneman often uses this seemingly simple math problem in
his lectures. A bat and a ball together cost $1.10. The bat costs a dol-
lar more than the ball. How much does the ball cost?

Your intuitive side may quickly tell you that the ball costs 10 cents.
Tempting answer, but wrong. In fact, if the ball costs 10 cents, that
would mean the bat costs one dollar more than that or $1.10, so the
two together would be $1.20. After you put a little more thought into
the problem, you realize the ball must have cost five cents. The point

is, it is important to distinguish between decisions that should be made by intuition and those that require careful thought and calculation.

I highly recommend you explore this field in more detail, as the scholars of behavioral finance have put years of sweat equity into fascinating research and study. Notably, I recommend *Choices, Values, and Frames* by Kahneman and Tversky; *Beyond Greed and Fear* by Hersh Shefrin; *Nudge*, written by Richard Thaler and Cass Sunstein; the investor behavior studies on 401(k)s by Shlomo Benartzi; articles, books and research by Meir Statman; *Against the Gods, The Remarkable Story of Risk* by Peter Bernstein, as a keen understanding of risk is more relevant than ever given the current economy; and *Investment Madness* by John Nofsinger, which is a good introductory book on behavioral finance written for the "lay" reader. Dr. Kahneman and I covered a wide array of behavioral finance concepts during our interview, and throughout the book, I'll explore some of these concepts and the impact they can have on your retirement. My time with Dr. Kahneman, as well as the vast body of work within behavioral finance, provided inspiration for the "ology" element of the book's retirement vision. *But what will that retirement look like?*

In the years following 9/11, Americans were afraid for their physical safety and survival. The passage of time—without further terrorist attacks in America—and recent economic events have shifted this focus. In assessing the salient issues in any given campaign, some political analysts have said, *"It's the economy, stupid."* Well, in the current environment, that might be refined to state, *"It's economic survival, stupid."* Millions of Americans who have never given much thought to the bottom of Maslow's Hierarchy of Needs are suddenly seeing that their nest eggs are wiped out, that their jobs have disappeared, that their homes are in jeopardy, and that any previous notions of retirement will clearly need to be rethought. In fact, many of them are seeing that it is not out of the realm of possibility that their largest headache could become simply putting groceries on the table and doing so for the foreseeable future. Millions of others are worried that one or more of these situations are just around the corner for them.

# Even with Your Best Efforts, This May Not Be Your Father's Retirement

Only in the last year did we finally surpass the fabled baby boom year of 1957 for record births, and only because the overall population is nearly double, not because families are having more babies than they did during the carefree days of the post-war era.[42] Now, more than 50 years later, many of those 77 million Baby Boomers begin their retirement journeys, and they are doing so on very precarious footing. Many Americans who were holding onto retirement dreams by a thread have seen that thread snap, and millions of others now need to proceed very carefully.

In the midst of one of the worst financial downturns in years, this generation of Baby Boomers is being tested like no other. Although most of us would not want to trade places with previous generations who suffered through the Great Depression, that generation did not have to overcome the challenges associated with living up to 30 years in retirement. The good news is that the products, programs, education, tools, and techniques are in place to help you succeed. And the successful retiree today needs to recognize a couple of important facts. First, skyrocketing house appreciation and double-digit returns are remnants from another time and not likely coming back anytime soon, if ever. Second, education and tools are only half of the puzzle. The other half will be composed of your willingness to embrace the new thinking and new behavior needed for a new era. Welcome to the world of *Retirementology*.

# Endnotes

1  ICMA-RC, "S&P 500 Index Historic Calendar Year Returns 1926-2007," May 2–8, 2008.

2  ICMA-RC, "S&P 500 Index Historic Calendar Year Returns 1926-2007," May 2–8, 2008.

3  Gallup Poll, "Americans: Economy Takes Precedence Over Environment," March 19, 2009.

4  Yahoo! Finance, Dow Jones Industrial Average (^DJI): Historical Prices, Dec. 31, 1990–Dec. 31, 1999.

5  *The Washington Post*, "401(k)s, Retirement Savings and the Financial Crisis," December 6, 2008; *The Wall Street Journal*, "The Great Recession: A Downturn Sized Up," July 28, 2009.

6  CNN Money, "Boomers: 30% underwater," February 25, 2009.

7  U.S. Bureau of Labor Statistics, "Economic News Releases: Mass Layoffs (Monthly)," December 22, 2009.

8  *The Wall Street Journal*, "1 in 4 Borrowers Under Water," November 24, 2009.

9  *USA Today*, "No one home: 1 in 9 housing units vacant," February 12, 2009.

10  San Francisco Gate, "Consumer confidence index hits record low," February 25, 2009.

11  McKinsey & Company, *The McKinsey Quarterly*, "Helping US consumers rethink retirement," May 2009.

12  Rasmussen Reports, "62% Say Today's Children Will Not Be Better Off Than Their Parents," October 3, 2009.

13  Dealscape, "Corporate defaults soar in March," April 7, 2009.

14  *Reuters*, "Employer's eye changes to 401(k) plans, study shows," June 22, 2009.

15  U.S. Census Bureau News, "Quarterly Retail E-commerce Sales," February 17, 2009.

16  Bloomberg, "Best Buy Drops After Cutting Forecast on Economy (Update2)," November 12, 2008.

17  Bloomberg, "Best Buy Drops After Cutting Forecast on Economy (Update2)," November 12, 2008.

18  *Chicago Tribune*, "Starbucks store closings," January 28, 2009.

19  Employee Benefit Research Institute, Issue Brief No. 326, "The Impact of the Recent Financial Crisis on 401(k) Account Balances," February 2009.

20  Report by Hewitt and Associates, Investopedia, "The Generation Gap," 2009.

21  Market Folly, "U.S. Savings Rate Rises: Temporary or Trend Reversal?" June 30, 2009.

22  McKinsey & Company, "Will U.S. consumer debt reduction cripple the recovery?" March 2009.

23  CBC News, "U.S. savings rate lowest since Depression," February 1, 2007.

24  *The Wall Street Journal*, "Big Slide in 401(k)s Spurs Calls for Change," January 8, 2009.

25  *The Wall Street Journal*, "Where Real Estate Is Still Hot," September 24, 2009.

26  *Reuters*, "An equal opportunity recession?" March 15, 2009.

27   The Heritage Foundation, "Fiscal Wake-Up Tour," 2009.

28   The Heritage Foundation, "The Obama Budget: Spending, Taxes, and Doubling the National Debt," March 16, 2009.

29   The Heritage Foundation, "The Obama Budget: Spending, Taxes, and Doubling the National Debt," March 16, 2009.

30   *Reuters*, "Is Obama planning a $3 trillion income tax increase?" November 17, 2009.

31   The Heritage Foundation, "The Obama Budget: Spending, Taxes, and Doubling the National Debt," March 16, 2009.

32   *Reuters*, "Obama seeks estate tax hike," May 11, 2009.

33   The Heritage Foundation, "The Obama Budget: Spending, Taxes, and Doubling the National Debt," March 16, 2009.

34   Center on Budget and Policy Priorities, "Tax Measures Help Balance State Budgets: A Common and Reasonable Response to Shortfalls," July 9, 2009.

35   TheTrumpet.com, "California Budget Crisis About to Affect People's Everyday Lives," January 21, 2009.

36   *Los Angeles Times*, "California faces financial meltdown as debt grows by $1.7m an hour," December 12, 2008.

37   *The Dallas Morning News*, "In bad economy, many Californians packing up and leaving," January 11, 2009.

38   National Coalition on Healthcare, "Insurance: Issue Areas," 2009.

39   Center on Budget and Policy Priorities, "Poverty Rose, Median Income Declined, and Job-Based Health Insurance Continued to Weaken in 2008; Recession Likely to Expand Ranks of Poor and Uninsured in 2009 and 2010," September 10, 2009.

40   The Pew Charitable Trusts, Financial Report: Entitlement Programs Underfunded by Trillions, December 16, 2008.

41   Kahneman, Daniel, and Amos Tversky, "Prospect Theory: An Analysis of Decision Under Risk," *Econometrica*, Vol. 47, No. 2 (March 1979), pp. 263–292.

42   *USA Today*, "Is this the next baby boom?" July 16, 2008.

# 1

## Great Expectations

## Man Walks into a Bank...

For millions of Baby Boomers preparing for retirement, we live in an era of what can best be described as *Romantic Illogic*. Consider the curious case of Timothy J. Bowers. In Columbus, Ohio, Mr. Bowers, age 62, couldn't find work, so he came up with a plan to make it through the next few years until he could collect Social Security. Mr. Bower's plan was out of the ordinary, to say the least. He robbed a bank and then handed the money over to a guard and waited for the police. Mr. Bowers passed a court-ordered psychological exam, and got his wish...he was sentenced to three years in prison, just enough time to take him to his Golden Years when he could collect his full Social Security check. The prosecutor was quoted as saying, *"It's not the financial plan I would have chosen, but at least it was a plan."*[1]

Before the Meltdown of 2008, very few Boomers had a retirement plan, but millions had retirement expectations. For example, 59% of the people in a survey said they expected to receive a pension check; however, only 41% knew of a pension to which they or their spouse were entitled.[2] Of the people who actually had a pension coming, the median expected annual pension was $20,000, but the median actual pension payout was only $8,340.[3] So did the bull market and strong economy create a quixotic-like disconnect between reality and fantasy? Why else would 50% of American workers say they expected to retire at 62, and 80% believed their standard of living would go up in retirement?[4] Why else would 70% of Boomers expect to leave an inheritance, not knowing if there was really any money to be left to their heirs?[5] After the Meltdown of 2008, you have to wonder: Who exhibited more irrational behavior...the bank-robbing Mr. Bowers who had a plan or the overconfident Boomer who had an expectation?

## The New McFear

When some of the world's largest companies and banks essentially vaporize or are forced to sell themselves in a matter of months, and the global economy appears to be sinking with record speed and harmony,[6] even the worst-conceived plans and the best-laid expectations can turn to fear, and suddenly no fear, for some of us, may seem irrational. In October 2008, Alan Greenspan, the former chairman of the U.S. Federal Reserve, confessed to Congress that he was *"shocked"* when the markets did not operate according to his lifelong expectations.[7] When things are tight and negative, economic news fills the headlines; people may tend to hold back on spending, pull money out of long-term investments, and potentially exacerbate the problem by holding onto their nest eggs for dear life. During the Meltdown of 2008, Bill Gross, considered the nation's most prominent bond investor, hypothetically equated the squeezed credit markets to being like a trip to a McDonald's drive-thru where one would pay at the first window, but could not be sure of actually getting their food at the second window. *"They are frozen in 'McFear,'"* said Gross.[8]

In a crisis, no story in the media seems out of bounds, which is why the media stokes fear. Case in point, remember the Avian flu, better known as the bird flu? In 2005, it was reported that an outbreak of the bird flu could kill anywhere between 2 million and

150 million people, but as of this writing there have been only 263 reported deaths caused by this disease.[9] Although the bird flu was indeed potentially dangerous, a measured, informative public discussion of the potential pandemic seemed nowhere to be found in the mass media. In the meantime, something much bigger was taking place, something that takes place every day, every month, every year in America, and yet it gets scant coverage as a rule. That something? The flu. That's right, the average, ordinary flu that we've probably all had a touch of at one time or another. In a flu season in the United States, an average of 36,000 people die of the flu or flu complications, and about 200,000 people are hospitalized.[10] That's more than 98 fatalities a day and well over 500 hospitalizations a day if the flu season were spread out over a year. Fortunately, bird flu hasn't come anywhere close to exacting that kind of toll, but as we all know, fear sells, and our perception of fear becomes reality.

As our economy suffered its own kind of flu, the headlines got worse and behavior became more irrational. After all, the economy is not only affected by the way people behave with their money, but it also affects the way people behave with their money. An example of this self-fulfilling prophecy is the hot dog stand story, which has been told in one form or another for well over 40 years. Here's the tale: Once upon a time, there was a man who ran a hot dog stand. This man ran one of the finest hot dog stands in the whole city and, strangely enough, he even used real meat in his sausages. People came from miles around to get his tasty hot dogs that were generously covered in onions and sauces. In fact, the man was so successful that he could afford to send his son to an Ivy League school. After graduation, the prodigal son came back home to visit his pop and took a look at the family business. *"Dad,"* he said, *"based on the current economic statistics, we're heading for a recession. You should really stop using all that sauce, and you dish out onions as if they were free. And you've been talking about expansion—adding another hot dog stand. Not the time to do that, Dad,"* he said. The father was torn. He was always generous to his customers, but his very bright son didn't get all that education for nothing. So, reluctantly, the father cut back on the sauces and onions. He held off on his expansion plans. His son even convinced him to buy a cheaper brand of hot dog. Although the son meant well, the timing of these cutbacks turned out to be just right, because right then the father's business took a real dive. After years of prospering as a street vendor, the hot dog man lost so many loyal customers to the competition, he had to close his stand. *The moral of the story*: The more you react to the fears and emotion of a recession, the more likely the recession will find you. Or...*what was the son thinking and what was the father feeling?*

## The Retirement Brain Game

At the risk of oversimplifying how the brain works, this complex machine can be divided into two cognitive systems. As mentioned in the introduction, the automatic system is subjective, intuitive, and instinctive, whereas the reflective system is objective, rational, and more deliberate. The automatic system is popularly coined the "right brain," whereas the reflective system is referred to as the "left brain." You've probably heard people say that they are either right-brain thinkers or left-brain thinkers; schools even build *whole-brained* curriculums to give equal weight to both sides of the way our brain functions. In the story you just read, the hot dog vendor approached his business with blind emotion, but his son actually evaluated the situation with what could be described as blind logic; both emotion and miscalculation can cloud our financial decision making. Although the right side of the brain is the culprit for most of our financial mistakes, the two sides together are often at odds, resulting in fear, dread, anxiety, euphoria, sadness, and conflict—essentially everything that makes us human. And because we are all human, let's have a little fun. Imagine the two sides of a Boomer's brain having a conversation. *What might they say about retirement?*

This is your brain. This is your brain on retirement.

**Right Brain:** Whoo hoo! Can't wait to retire.

**Left Brain:** Retire? What exactly is the plan?

**Right Brain:** Travel. Beach. Golf. But not just for two weeks, for the rest of my life.

**Left Brain:** Okay, so tell me. Have you thought about the numbers?

**Right Brain:** 18—as in holes a day.

**Left Brain:** You are irrational.

**Right Brain:** I am exuberant.

**Left Brain:** Seriously.

**Right Brain:** Okay, we'll sell the house.

**Left Brain:** Underwater. With three mortgages.

**Right Brain:** Investments?

**Left Brain:** Down 40% since the meltdown.

**Right Brain:** What about our nest egg?

**Left Brain:** I told you to start 25 years ago, Mr. Procrastinator.

**Right Brain:** We can always count on family.

**Left Brain:** Not returning calls.

**Right Brain:** Government?

**Left Brain:** Have you seen the news?

**Right Brain:** You're freaking me out.

**Left Brain:** The technical term for that is ohnosis.

---

**OHNOSIS:** [oh-**noh**-sis]

Realizing that you really should have started planning for retirement years ago. *After John completed the online retirement calculator, he was struck with a severe case of ohnosis.*

---

Expectations are driven by a number of behaviors, and from behavioral finance we examine a few concepts in this chapter, such as *overconfidence* and *illusion of control*, that helped shape high expectations for Boomers prior to the meltdown. I'll review a familiar concept called *procrastination* and a not-so-familiar concept called the *recency effect*, both of which will most likely continue to influence, and even plague, investor behavior in the post-meltdown era.

**Procrastination**—Psychological bias that keeps people from engaging in the day-to-day activities that could result in a long-term benefit. One way it manifests itself is the way people fail to sign up for their 401(k) accounts when they become eligible, which is often months after starting with a company. They become comfortable with their take-home pay and don't believe they can cut into it at all to fund a retirement that's decades away. So they put off funding their retirement, spend all their pay, and do nothing to maximize their wealth.

**Overconfidence**—Actions based on an exaggerated estimation of one's knowledge, skill, and good fortune. Even if a person did nothing to make that investment successful, other than buy it, he may think that he's learned something important about how to make money in the market and try to apply that learning to future investments. The result is that the investor believes he knows more than he actually does and can control more than he actually can.

**Illusion of Control**—The tendency for investors to believe that they can control or influence an outcome over which they have absolutely no control.

**Recency Effect**—Giving more importance to recent events than to those events that took place further in the past. Investors who were recently stung by the market, as was the case in the fall of 2008, were cautious about getting back in during the bull market that took place in the spring and summer of 2009.

### *The Procrastinator's Plight*

*Procrastination*. The word conjures up images of laziness and detachment. And *procrastination* is a big reason why retirement expectations are not met. *Procrastination* isn't necessarily a problem relegated solely to the unmotivated among us. It is a psychological bias that affects millions and can keep us from building a retirement nest egg. We all want to make timely, well-thought-out financial decisions, but *procrastination* lurks in the shadows waiting to derail our retirement dream.

Consider for a moment our increasingly complicated, ever-changing, fast-paced world. It is one that differs dramatically from the society we inherited from our parents and grandparents. Despite this radical technological evolution, our natural tendency is to keep things the way they were. And it's an understandable reaction considering the blitz of changes constantly demanding our attention. After all, it's much easier to do nothing rather than alter one more detail in our already busy and overburdened lives. In fact, *Seinfeld*, one of the most successful situation comedies of all time, was a self-proclaimed show about *doing nothing*. Truth is, most of us prefer to *do nothing*. For example, your car may no longer be exactly what you want, but keeping it is easier than looking for a new one. *Do nothing*. Your job may not be as satisfying as you would like, but the daunting task of searching for a new one may be even less appealing. *Do nothing*. Fifty-three percent of workers in the U.S. have less than $25,000 in savings and investments,[11] but what will most of them do differently going forward? *Nothing*.

Many people acknowledge that *procrastination* plays a major role in keeping them from starting to plan for retirement. Why? You may be overwhelmed by the notion of retirement; afraid you'll make too many mistakes in retirement planning; have too many competing priorities; or just lack a sense of urgency. According to a survey conducted on behalf of the Securities Industry and Financial Markets Association, the majority of adults would choose to receive financial advice over the advice of a personal trainer, interior designer, or fashion consultant, if given the opportunity.[12] But here's the conundrum: LIMRA, a financial services research firm, reports only 15% of consumers said they had consulted with an adviser during the economic crisis. Whereas 85% procrastinated and did nothing, even during a crisis, two-thirds of those investors who did seek financial advice during the crisis felt reassured and were glad they acted.[13]

### The Cost of Waiting

A consistent theme among our age 60+ focus group participants was regret over not starting to plan for retirement sooner. Although better late than never is always a worthwhile notion, urging your children to start planning for their financial future as early as possible is one of the most important pieces of advice you can pass along to your family. Let's take a look at the advantage of starting early and the disadvantage of procrastinating. Table 1.1 illustrates the potential cost of waiting to invest. Susan invests $10,000 for 10 years and stops. Sally waits 10 years and then invests $10,000 for 25 years. Assuming a hypothetical rate of return of 8% for both, Susan will have more money than Sally despite investing significantly less money upfront.

**Table 1.1   SUSAN VERSUS SALLY: The Power of Time (Hypothetical Example)**

|                   | Susan             | Sally              |
| ----------------- | ----------------- | ------------------ |
| Age 31–40         | $10,000 per year  | $0 per year        |
| Age 41–65         | $0 per year       | $10,000 per year   |
| Total Investment  | $100,000          | $250,000           |
| Value at Age 65   | $1,071,477        | $789,544           |

This chart is hypothetical and for illustrative purposes only. The hypothetical rates of return shown in this chart are not guaranteed and should not be viewed as indicative of the past or future performance of any particular investment. This chart assumes a hypothetical rate of return of 8%.

Think about it. Have you ever heard people say they were glad that they waited years, even decades, to begin planning for their retirement? Many people acknowledge that *procrastination* plays a major role in keeping them from doing a better job of planning for their retirement. There are so many choices and unknowns that it is often easier to focus on the more immediate concerns of daily living.

> *"What I have on the list, I think my biggest obstacle is me, quite honestly. I just feel kind of overwhelmed by the topic. There is almost so much information about ways to prepare and invest in retirement, that to me it overwhelms me and I shut down. It's always I'll look another day, I'll check into that tomorrow. I have no doubt that I am my biggest obstacle to achieving great success in retirement."*

—Male Focus Group Participant

Some investors take the opposite approach. Rather than proscrastinate, they invest immediately, without making more patient choices for the future. For example, someone offered the choice between receiving $100 today or $110 tomorrow might be tempted to take the money today. But if that same person were asked to choose between receiving $100 a year from now, or receiving $110 in a year and one day, he would likely prefer to wait the extra day for the larger payoff.[14] Instant gratification can also be a factor in the behavior of procrastination; in some cases, people will do what is necessary to get something they want immediately but are not inclined to start acting on something that may get them what they're after 20–30 years down the road. Behavioral finance studies have been conducted with fruit and chocolate, as well as "low brow" and "high brow" movies.[15] In both studies, people will typically choose chocolate and "low brow" movies today, and fruit and "high brow" movies tomorrow.[16] When it comes to retirement planning, making impatient choices and opting for instant gratification today, while delaying patient, even better and better-for-you choices for tomorrow can affect our investment decisions. For example, rather than being patient and riding out paper losses from investment downturns, people may act without thinking and make investment decisions that aren't prudent.

Failure to follow through once a decision has been reached is also a common factor in procrastination. And it's an easy one to relate to. Take joining a gym, for example. When buying gym memberships, I think many people tend to be overeager and possibly naïve in their forecasting. A discounted monthly payment may seem like a smarter move than a higher per visit fee, but if you don't show up, the per-visit fee is a better value. I had a friend with a very busy schedule who was excited about joining *24-Hour Fitness*® because he could go any-time—even in the middle of the night to work out. *"Problem is,"* he said, *"I never got the urge to go to the gym in the middle of the night—so I never got to the gym."* But he kept making his so-called discounted monthly payment, which was pulled directly from his checking account.

We live in a busy world that's constantly pulling us in different directions. There's no question that most people want to take actions that will benefit their financial bottom line, but they often do not finish the task. When faced with making an important or complex decision, it's not unusual for investors to either keep things the way they are or delay making a decision until later. This behavior is particularly damaging to retirement and can be seen in the way many workers fail to take advantage of company-sponsored retirement plans. Despite easy access to investment information, many employees have difficulty taking action even though they understand the need to join their retirement plan, choose allocations, and increase their contribution rates.

### The Overconfident Investor

Although *procrastination* traps us in the gap between thinking and doing, **overconfidence** tricks us into thinking we are better than we actually are at performing a particular task. Investors who suffer from *overconfidence* have a tendency to believe that their forecasts are right and that more knowledge will only solidify their beliefs. But the fact is that more knowledge can sometimes be contradictory to what an investor already knows. Although common sense dictates that learning more about an investment would naturally make a person a better investor, a behavioral finance concept called the **illusion of control** dictates that's not necessarily the case.

Rooted in *overconfidence*, the *illusion of control* tricks people into thinking they have more control over an outcome than they actually do. An example is the documented fact that if you ask someone to bet on which side a coin will land on, the person will bet more money on the side it *didn't* land on the time before. The problem with this thinking is that the coin obviously has two sides, and there's a 50% chance a tossed coin will land on one side each time the coin is flipped. Like the coin toss, investors frequently use last year's result to make this year's investment decisions without properly analyzing the information. Our minds are calibrated to believe only what we will accept, and we are often surprised when predictions prove not to be right. We know the past, especially the recent past, like a stock's year-to-date earnings, but there's so much more to know to make an educated investment decision. Based on what we do know, many of us have a tendency to believe that we have more control over an outcome than we really do. Witness the all-star baseball player who has a superstition of tapping his spikes before entering the batter's box. He may claim that such a ritual helps him succeed, but if he has a .300 batting average, that means he does not succeed 70% of the time. Although such an average is quite impressive in baseball, the batter's ability and mastery of his skill have a lot more to do with his success than the superstition that gives him the *illusion of control*.

### Are you overconfident?

Before we continue, answer this question: How would you rate your driving skill? Compared to other drivers you encounter on the road, are you

- Above average
- Average
- Below average

If you're like most people, you answered that you are *above average*. When we asked our focus group participants this question, 90% of the room stated they were above average, but given that our focus group was composed of a cross section of America, it is very unlikely that 90% of the room was average or above. Just like driving, many Americans may be overconfident that their investment decisions are prudent. For example, during the bull market, some investors thought they knew best where to put their money, and they continue to think that to this day. In the '90s, they believed it was tech stocks; in the late 2000s, it seems to have been target date funds and home equity. CNBC's two-part special *House of Cards*, which aired in January of 2009 and detailed the financial meltdown that was triggered by the bursting of the real estate bubble, featured an interview with Alan Greenspan. During the interview, Greenspan stated that all the people who'd invested heavily in real estate or subprime mortgage-backed securities thought they would get out of those positions ahead of everyone else. But many of these people—among them some of the brightest minds on Wall Street—did not get out ahead of the others and, in fact, they were holding worthless paper when the meltdown happened.

## The Nearsighted Investor

*Overconfidence* in both bull and bear markets can, in part, be attributed to a behavioral finance concept known as the **recency effect**. When people look back over a short period of time, they remember the good things as well as the struggles. In investing terms, if a person looks back a quarter or two and sees his accounts have grown in value, he's likely to invest even more, overloading investments in equities without maintaining a well-balanced portfolio. Conversely, when investors experience something like the Meltdown of 2008, they may react to it in the exact opposite way, perhaps being overly conservative with their investments. If we do not experience anything like the meltdown in the next year or so, investors will be less influenced by it. The *recency effect* dictates that experiences happening in real time affect behavior in real time, like an economic boom. Witness the American economy since the Baby Boomers came along: For the most part, the American economy and quality of life have risen consistently. After the meltdown, the relatively carefree days of the Dow at 14,000 (that happened just 50 weeks earlier) suddenly seemed like a distant memory. A new reality was upon Americans, and they reacted by looking at their finances in a whole new way. But how many react by *permanently* looking at their finances in a whole new way? *"We will see people pulling in their belts for 1 or 2 years,"* insists Augustana College history professor and American consumer credit expert Lendol Calder. *"And then it will be back to where we left off."*[17]

When people are faced with a new reality, like losing their nest egg very quickly, they don't always react as rationally as they should. Long-term knowledge and even experience is tossed out the window in favor of a reaction to short-term stimulus. The result is that businesses and individuals alike are doing what they can to cut back on expenses and even hoard money. At some point the headlines will stop trumpeting bad economic news, regardless of how good or bad the economy is at that point. At that time the hurt and anguish that was brought about by the meltdown will recede, and people will become more engaged about who's the next *American Idol* than what they do with their dollars.

# Improve Your Retirementology IQ

A century and a half ago, Charles Dickens wrote *Great Expectations*, about a young man named Pip who took the occasion of sudden wealth to eschew his working class roots and move up in London society. Like the mysterious benefactor who eventually bestowed riches upon Pip, many people expect to have their own retirement dreams fulfilled by other mysterious benefactors in the form of pension checks, lottery tickets, and rich uncles—great expectations of travel, leisure, devoting time and money to a charitable cause, winter homes and summer homes, time with friends and family, and possibly leaving a noble amount of money behind for those who are most important. In fact, when asked what is the most practical manner to accumulate $500,000 for retirement, 27% of respondents said winning the lottery or sweepstakes.[18] Could it be that the survey was taken among characters in Dickens' novel?

A meltdown has a way of changing expectations—even for a generation high on promise and light on planning.

Take a moment to evaluate what you're thinking in this post-meltdown era. How well did you deal with your fears? Did you lose sleep? Did you develop a nervous tick? Did you watch the markets every day? Did you make any financial moves out of panic? It's likely that a lot of the things you did do in response to the economic downturn you did because you didn't know what else to do. Modifying your expectations doesn't have to mean abandoning your retirement dreams—just rethinking them. Here are two takeaways to consider to get started on rethinking expectations.

### Conduct a Personal Retirement Assessment

What do you want? What do you need? What are you willing to do, to sacrifice, to achieve these material things? You have to be willing to think about opportunity costs, like if you'll be happy driving a less flashy car today to drive a golf cart every day in retirement. Or if you're okay raising your family in your present house so that you might have a winter house in retirement. Some people simply can't get past immediate gratification, whereas others look at all the issues and realize that they can put some things off now for the possibility of a secure retirement. Remember, even small decisions can make a big difference in your retirement planning, and retirement is ultimately affected by many monetary decisions throughout your life, like starting to plan ahead as early as possible.

### *Reevaluate Retirement Expectations*

What's your retirement dream? Would you like to retire to a big house overlooking a lake and the mountains where the view is always beautiful and you can decide whether you want to golf, ski, or go sailing every morning when you wake up? Everyone's dream is unique, but reality can get in the way of a dream, even for the wealthiest retiree. What do you really want? And what will it take to get there? If it's a winter house in Arizona or Florida, you have to know approximately how much it will cost. If it's a boat so that you can travel the world, you need to have an idea of how much you'll need. Be realistic. Be honest with yourself. Be as objective as you can be, and leave nothing out when you make your checklist...right down to how many golf balls you'll need because you always hook your driver into the water. Improving your Retirementology IQ often begins by examining your options and feelings *before* the unthinkable happens. You may feel like the unthinkable has already happened. Keep in mind that, historically, the economy and markets have been cyclical. Learn from today, but don't lose your long-term retirement perspective.

*"This time it's different"*—perhaps four of the most dangerous words in investing. No matter what the political or economic climate may be like, investing always involves risks. Consider the growth of the S&P 500 Index since 1926 (see Figure 1.1). Like many investments, stocks have experienced some severe declines, as well as dramatic growth—despite wars and meltdowns. *What will the next headline be?*

Mark Twain said, *"Climate is what we expect, weather is what we get."* When it comes to expectations, the best thing you can do is check them at the door and plan for all kinds of weather in retirement.

## UNREALISTIC LIFESTYLE EXPECTATIONS MAKE A HAPPY RETIREMENT IMPOSSIBLE.

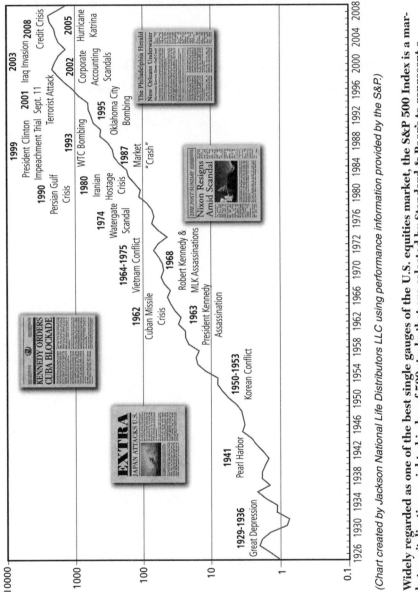

*(Chart created by Jackson National Life Distributors LLC using performance information provided by the S&P.)*

Widely regarded as one of the best single gauges of the U.S. equities market, the S&P 500 Index is a market capitalization-weighted index of 500 stocks that are selected by Standard & Poor's to represent a broad array of large companies in leading industries. This chart represents the growth of a hypothetical

$1 invested in the S&P 500 from 1926–2008, during which time the Index experienced an average annual return of 9.62%. The S&P 500 is an unmanaged, broad-based index and is not available for direct investment. Past performance is no guarantee of future results.

## It really isn't different.

A quick history of events that shaped the political and economic climate in the United States shows us that turmoil is nothing new to the financial markets.

| | | |
|---|---|---|
| 1950 Korean "police" action begins | 1971 Wage and price freezes | 1992 President Bush signs NAFTA |
| 1951 Excess Profits Tax | 1972 Largest U.S. trade deficit ever | 1993 1st Democrat in White House in 12 years |
| 1952 Government takes over steel mills | 1973 Oil prices skyrocket, energy crisis | 1994 One of the worst years on record for bonds |
| 1953 Russia explodes H-bomb | 1974 Watergate forces Nixon resignation | 1995 Dow breaks 5000 |
| 1954 President Eisenhower suffers heart attack | 1975 Clouded economic prospects | 1996 1st Democrat re-elected to White House since FDR |
| 1956 Crisis in Suez | 1976 Economic recovery stalls | |
| 1958 Recession | 1977 Market slumps | 1998 Markets on roller coaster ride |
| 1959 Cuba falls to Castro | 1978 Turmoil in Iran | 1999 "Y2K" concerns |
| 1960 Russia downs U-2 plane | 1979 Oil prices skyrocket | 2000 "Dot.com" uncertainties |
| 1961 Berlin Wall erected | 1980 Iranian hostage crisis, inflation | 2001 September 11 terrorist attacks |
| 1962 Cuban Missile Crisis | 1981 Record-high interest rates | 2002 Corporate accounting scandals |
| 1963 JFK assassinated | 1982 Worst recession in 40 years | 2003 U.S. invasion of Iraq |
| 1965 Civil rights issue explodes | 1984 Record federal deficits | 2004 Tsunami in Indonesia |
| 1966 Vietnam War escalates | 1985 Money tightens – markets fall | 2005 Hurricanes Katrina, Rita, and Wilma |
| 1967 Inner city riots | 1986 Dow nears 2000 | 2006 Democrats control Congress for first time in 12 years |
| 1968 Martin Luther King, Robert Kennedy assassinations | 1987 Bull market crashes on October 19th | |
| 1969 Money tightens – markets fall | 1990 Persian Gulf crisis | 2007 U.S. enters into a recession |
| 1970 Cambodia invaded, Vietnam War spreads | 1991 Soviet Union collapses | 2008 Credit crisis hits Wall Street |

(Source: History.com, "History timelines... The History Beat," 2009.)

**Figure 1.1  Is it really different this time?**

# Endnotes

1  *The New York Times,* "Just Asking to Be Caught, Thief Solves Joblessness," October 13, 2006.

2  *Consumer Reports,* "Are You Ready to Retire?" October 2008.

3  Tiburon Strategic Advisors, "Consumer Wealth, Liquefaction, & the Retirement Income Challenge Research Report – Key Highlights," February 29, 2008.

4  *USA Today,* "Boomers' eagerness to retire could cost them," January 13, 2008; MSN Money, "9 dumb moves to ruin your retirement," October 22, 2007.

5  Gallup News Service, "Most Americans Don't Expect to Receive an Inheritance," August 27, 2007.

6  PBS, "Frontline: Inside the Meltdown," February 17, 2009.

7  *The Wall Street Journal,* "Greenspan 'Shocked' to Find Flaw in Ideology," October 23, 2008.

8  PIMCO Investment Outlook, "Nothing to Fear but McFear Itself," October 2008.

9  ABC News, "How Many People Could Bird Flu Kill?" September 30, 2005; World Health Organization, Cumulative Number of Confirmed Human Cases of Avian Influenza A/(H5N1) Reported to WHO, December 21, 2009.

10  Centers for Disease Control and Prevention, "Estimating Deaths from Seasonal Influenza in the United States," September 4, 2009; Centers for Disease Control and Prevention, "Seasonal Influenza – Associated Hospitalizations in the United States," September 8, 2009.

11  Employee Benefit Research Institute, "The 2009 Retirement Confidence Survey: Economy Drives Confidence to Record Lows; Many Looking to Work Longer," No. 328, April 2009.

12  Securities Industry and Financial Markets Association, "Survey: Most Crave Financial Advice Over Personal Trainer, Fashion Consultant," October 3, 2007.

13  LIMRA, "Consumer Views on the Fall of 2008," 2008.

14  McClure, Samuel M., David I. Laibson, George Loewenstein, and Jonathan D. Cohen, "Separate Neural Systems Value Immediate and Delayed Monetary Rewards," October 15, 2004.

15  Read, Daniel, and Barbara van Leeuwen, "Predicting Hunger: The Effects of Appetite and Delay on Choice," Organizational Behavior and Human Decision Processes, Vol. 76, Issue 2, pgs. 189–205, November 1998.

16  Read, Daniel, George Loewenstein, and Roy F. Baumeister, <u>Time and Decision: Economic and Psychological Perspectives on Intertemporal Choice</u>, Russell Sage Foundation Publications, 2003.

17  *The New York Times,* "The Last Temptation of Plastic," December 7, 2008.

18  MSN Money, "Why poor people win the lottery," May 9, 2008.

# 2

# Gold Dust on Sushi

---

**DAMNESIA:** [dam-*nee*-zhuh]

Prepurchase state of forgetting how badly it will feel when the damn credit card bill arrives. *James later blamed the damnesia when he plopped his Amex down for the full-carbon mountain bike.*

---

When they were seemingly on top of the economic world during the 1980s, the Japanese would routinely sprinkle gold dust on their sushi. Gold leaf flakes were sometimes used instead of dry seaweed to wrap the rice,[1] and amazingly, the world record for spending on a sushi roll comes in at $83,500, paid in Tokyo in January 1992.[2] A recent Japanese film, "Bubble e Go! Time Machine wa Drum Shiki," which roughly translates to "Back to the Bubble," revisits some of the common behaviors of the 1980 boom showcasing the extravagant practice of drinking green tea and sake with gold leaf flakes.[3] The fad extended to other types of cuisine, including omelets, curries, and ice cream. Not to be left out, a New York restaurant began serving $1,000 sushi rolls wrapped in edible gold leafs.[4] Indeed, sushi trends were a pretty good barometer for what was going on with the rest of consumer spending.

After decades of spending on fine dining, bigger houses, luxurious cars, electronic gadgets, expensive clothing, and all sorts of other niceties, America's Baby Boomers now have an embarrassment of riches when it comes to material goods, *but very little cash.* The solution was simple: credit. Americans had more material wealth than they'd ever had, in spite of the fact that they had little in the way of actual cash savings. They were seeing their homes and other investments balloon in paper value. Then, they were getting home equity loans to pay for renovations, kids' college tuition, a dream vacation, or even a new car. No sooner had they spent that newly created home equity, than they discovered the house had appreciated yet another 10%—providing further appreciation.[5]

The home equity loan wasn't the only easy credit, though. For years, they were bringing in the mail every day to find about a half-dozen credit card applications with teaser offers enticing them to move revolving balances to these cards. As of 2008, Americans held more than $850 billion in credit card debt; that's four times the credit card debt Americans held as recently as 1990.[6] The result has been a widespread case of musical credit cards among the consumers who did hold revolving debt. Thirty-five million of them make only the minimum payment each month or move their balances from one card to another with a low teaser rate that would balloon to something like prime plus 12% after a few months.[7]

*"People have come to view credit as savings,"* says Michelle Jones, vice president at the Consumer Credit Counseling Service of Greater Atlanta.[8] Easy credit kept the cycle going, and rising home values kept Americans feeling rich. Their behavior, however, didn't make them rich. Consumers often treated the simple act of throwing down a card as the only thing between them and whatever they wanted at a particular time. Lunch? Put it on the card. Plane ticket? On the card, please. Big screen television? That's what the card is for, right? What some people never really learned was that the interest they were paying by rolling over that balance from month to month could make that $5 lunch cost $205 when it was finally paid off. The $205 plane ticket may cost $2,005, and the $2,005 big screen TV could cost…well, you get the idea.

Too many of us were putting money into someone else's pocket at an alarming rate by spending much more on a product than it was worth. Think of a chess player who continually gives up a bishop or a rook to capture a pawn; he won't be very successful in the long term.

The result? In 2008, Americans carried $2.56 trillion in consumer debt—22% of that has been incurred just since 2000.[9] The picture that's painted by these facts is that Americans now must set aside 14.5% of their disposable income *just to service their debt.*[10]

By comparison to the federal government, however, American consumers are so frugal they could be called fiscally responsible. At the end of the government's fiscal year on September 30, 2009, the feds are running an incredible $1.42 trillion budget deficit, which is triple what it was a year before[11] and bigger than the entire national debt as recently as 1984.[12] So how big is the national debt now? How does $12.3 trillion hit you?[13] *So how many of our tax dollars are going to have to go toward just servicing that debt?*

Many Americans who live well are so deep in debt that their quality of life would drop significantly in just a few weeks if the paychecks stopped coming in. According to one national study, 50% of Americans say they're only one month—two paychecks—away from not being able to meet their financial obligations.[14] More than half of those people, 28% of the total respondents, couldn't survive financially for more than two weeks if they were suddenly without their present regular income.[15] And before you think this issue concerns only lower socio-economic Americans, think again. Twenty-nine percent of the "mass affluent," earning more than $100,000 per year, wouldn't be able to meet financial obligations a month after losing their jobs.[16] So how did we get here? What's behind the *carpe diem* spending mentality?

## America's Spending Boom

Before the meltdown, it didn't matter as much if we were a paycheck away from disaster. In recent years, most people didn't even realize they were flirting with disaster, or if they did, they looked the other way. Let's take a glimpse at some of the extravagance that underscored America's *carpe diem* spending mentality.

- **Luxuries became everyday necessities.**
  - Overspending Boomers might regularly drop $5 or $10 a day on intakes of latté, cappuccino, espresso, mocha, macchiato, and a multitude of other beverages, as Starbucks sales grew and stock went above $30 a share at the high point in 2007.[17] Not bad, considering Starbucks stock traded at about 70¢ per share in the summer of 1992.[18] One of our focus group participants noted, *"People go to Starbucks, put the card through, get a $5 drink and don't know how much they spent."* Another stated, *"I have a friend who goes to Starbucks, and it makes me cringe because he is in debt a lot. He has a $4,000 Starbucks bill. And he juggles his credit cards."*
  - Big-screen television sales shot up 300–400% from 2006 to 2007, as unit sales for the LCD TV category were up 74%.[19]
  - Nearly one-third of U.S. adults went boating in 2006. Sales of new boats nationwide were $15 billion in 2006, a record high.[20]
- **No vehicle was too lavish, big, or brawny.**
  - One successful Hummer dealer spent $7.5 million on a new 34,000-square-foot showroom in a wealthy suburb of St. Louis and turned 60 acres into a rough-terrain track to test drive his Hummers. This dealership was selling 70 new Hummers a month—priced from $30,000 to $100,000.[21] Stories and features about exotic cars were also prevalent in magazines, as witnessed in a December 2005 *Forbes* magazine article that spotlighted such exotic cars as the $1.2 million Veyron 16.4, the $654,000 SSC Ultimate Aero, and the $285,000 Lambourghini Murciélago. *Would any of those make a great holiday gift?*
- **No party was too lavish.**
  - Dozens of overprivileged kids had their coming-of-age extravaganzas captured on MTV's hit series "My Super Sweet 16." The show follows teenagers as they painstakingly plan their elaborate celebrations, which cost as much as $200,000. There are tears and tantrums and nouveau-riche displays of conspicuous consumption. Marissa, a daddy's girl from Arizona, dyes her two poodles pink, so they'll match

her dress.[22] The other end of birthday party economics revealed that 21% of Chuck E. Cheese customers spent between $225 and $300 on parties for their kids. A vast majority of that spending—62%—went toward games rather than food.[23]

– Steven Schwarzman, CEO of Blackstone, threw himself a $5 million 60th birthday party at the Park Avenue Armory in February 2007. It featured marching band entertainment and a 50-foot silkscreen re-creation of his apartment.[24]

And it wasn't just the conspicuously wealthy who were bitten by the overindulgence bug. Americans of all socio-economic levels joined in. People who appeared as if they weren't sure where they would sleep at night were spending their days chatting away on their cell phones or listening to iPods. Don't believe that one? Take a stroll down Santa Monica, California's 3rd Street Promenade sometime, where I have seen throngs of vagrants find a welcoming environment, or the backyard of the typical American middle-class neighborhood.

Before the Meltdown of 2008, America was booming. Just for fun, let's listen in on an imaginary conversation during a backyard barbeque, circa 2005....

**Jim:** *Nice place, Jack.*

**Jack:** *Thanks. It took a long time to finish the renovation, but it was worth it.*

**Jim:** *What took so long?*

**Jack:** *You mean besides my wife's inability to make a decision on the color of the deck stain? And the barbeque being on back order for, well, forever? All good now, though. Adds value to the home, too, right?*

**Jim:** *Yep, that's what the TV shows call curb appeal. Like putting money in your bank account. We put in some landscaping, too. My wife wanted a water feature, which seemed silly to me until I realized I could use that against her and get the putting green I always wanted.*

**Jack:** *Nice. You can settle in on a Saturday afternoon with a beer and work on the short game.*

**Jim:**   *You know it. That's what I did today.*

**Jack:**  *I played Xbox with my son. I swear; kids are hard-wired to play those video games.*

**Jim:**   *We're a ways away from the video games. I'll have to come down to your house over the next couple years and practice, so my boys don't wipe the floor with me. Who knows what they'll come up with next?*

**Jack:**  *Whatever it is, you can bet my kids will have to have it, and we'll ante up. I just wish they'd come up with a game to get them moving while they're playing. I hate to see them sitting so long. Hey, how about a margarita?*

**Jim:**   *Sounds good. That looks like a blender from the future. High tech.*

# America's Spending Bust

From boom to bust, the days of wine and roses came to a crashing halt, and a generation of spenders woke up with one giant hangover, starting in 2008. As comedian Jackie Mason said, *"Right now I have enough money to last me the rest of my life, unless I buy something."*[25]

- Four in ten Americans now feel buyer's remorse—wishing they had spent less money during good times and put more away over several years.[26]
- Average American household credit card debt equals $8,565, up almost 15% in 2008 since 2000.[27]
- Americans have $10.5 trillion in just mortgage debt since the end of 2007, more than double the $4.8 trillion in 2002.[28]

- **The big buzz kill.**
  - According to a survey by Lightspeed Research, 60% of Americans have scaled back on fancy or expensive coffee in the past six months; 43% of those completing the survey indicated that they frequented Starbucks the most.[29]
  - For the first time, annual sales of flat panel TVs looked to decline from $24.4 billion in 2008 to $21.8 billion in 2009.[30]

- **Hummers not humming.**
  - Hummer's U.S. sales tumbled 51% in 2008—the worst drop in the industry.[31] *"It's a brand that represents a lot of what people want to get away from,"* said Rebecca Lindland, an analyst with the research firm I.H.S. Global Insight. *"Even if gas prices are lower, it still kind of radiates conspicuous consumption."*[32]

- **The party is over.**
  - "My Super Sweet 16" has been canceled and many parents find themselves relying on the "less is more" ethos this time around, and parents are increasingly gravitating to lower-cost shopping options, from Wal-Mart to secondhand stores.[33]

- **Back to basics.**

  After the meltdown, necessity and luxury were redefined, as many consumers got back to basics.[34]
  - 57% of people bought less expensive brands or shopped more at discount stores.
  - 28% of people cut back spending on alcohol or cigarettes.
  - 24% of people reduced or canceled cable or satellite TV subscriptions.
  - 22% of people changed to a less expensive cell phone plan or canceled service.
  - 21% of people made plans to plant a vegetable garden.
  - 20% started doing yard work or home repairs that they used to pay for.
  - 16% of people held a garage sale or sold items on the Internet.
  - 10% of people had a friend or relative move in or moved in with them.
  - 2% of people rented out to a boarder.

Now, let's listen in on that imaginary conversation at a backyard barbeque, circa 2009....

**Jim:** *I understand your house is on the market.*

**Jack:** *It was, but we accepted an offer yesterday. But don't tell anyone. The neighbors won't be happy with the price. We're losing a little, but I think we'll make it up when we buy again somewhere.*

**Jim:**   *You just wanted out, huh?*

**Jack:**  *Well, after we put the pool in….*

**Jim:**   *I thought you loved your pool.*

**Jack:**  *It's a lot of work. We weren't even going to fill it up this summer.*

**Jim:**   *I'm sure the new owner will.*

**Jack:**  *Don't be so sure. The guy's a landlord—he bought the house to rent it out. Might fill in the pool.*

**Jim:**   *Ooooh, really? Where are you moving?*

**Jack:**  *Wherever a job takes me. It's sort of one project at a time. First was selling the house; tomorrow is my youngest daughter's birthday party.*

**Jim:**   *What are you gonna do for that? Chuck E. Cheese again or Build-a-Bear? That's what my daughter has been screaming for.*

**Jack:**  *No, I think we're just going to have some of her friends over. You know, play some games.*

**Jim:**   *I hear ya. I took my son's party to the amusement park a few weeks ago…should've taken out an installment loan. Wow!*

**Jack:**  *Yea. I'm going to miss the neighborhood.*

**Jim:**   *Well, don't lose touch.*

**Jack:**  *I won't. Let's get a beer.*

**Jim:**   *Or two.*

# The Retirement Brain Game

**Mental Accounting**—So we spend too much and save and invest too little. And when we do this, we often make mistakes, even though our intentions are good. Behavioral finance studies show that some financial errors can be attributed to a behavior known as *mental accounting*. Imagine an inbox inside your head where you store accounting files, and you label your mental folders, assign them values, and make financial decisions based on them. For example, *emergency money, bill money, birthday money, gas money, fun money*—you get the idea. In and of itself, categorizing money is not a problem; however, as we will see, *mental accounting* can become a detriment when it influences the way we spend, save, and invest money. *Mental accounting* can influence decisions in unexpected ways and can keep us from maximizing the dollars in each account.

**Layering**—In behavioral finance, *layering* refers to the way people treat their money when they're not dealing with actual money, but rather proxies for money. Using checks, credit cards, or room numbers at the hotel while lounging about the pool are all ways that consumers can create psychological layers of distance between themselves and their money. Or people may give a green light to an hourly fee without knowing the total amount of cost. All these different ways to pay make money more and more opaque to consumers and provide perfect examples of *layering*.

### Tic-Tac-Dough

In one of our focus groups, a participant told us she was well aware of the potential damage of revolving debt with exorbitant interest rates. And she proudly proclaimed that she had no such debt. She told us that she paid her monthly bills on time, paid off the balances of her department store credit cards, and even kept a savings account that she only touched for emergencies. But as our research team continued quizzing her, she revealed, almost as an aside, that she kept a balance on her VISA, *"Because that was different."* What's different? Granted, in this economy, more people are feeling the need to keep a "rainy day" account in case of job loss, which is a perfectly rational idea on the surface. But does this make good financial sense when you drill down? Keeping a "rainy day" account in a low-interest savings vehicle, while still paying on another account, like a high-interest credit card or loan, can be a losing proposition because of the potential cost of that high interest. When you crunch the numbers, you may see that you are better served paying the high interest account in full with the savings. For example, if she is paying 16% a year in interest on her credit card but earning only 2% on her emergency fund, that's a yearly loss of $140 for every $1,000 spent. It adds up. The way we mentally account for our money, however, can prohibit us from parting with the safety net. The good news is that **mental account-ing** can be used in a positive manner. I'll discuss how you can turn the pitfalls of *mental accounting* into a benefit, and for the sake of this discussion, I'll refer to that as *mental budgeting*.

One measure that proves useful in understanding how we mentally account for money is how transparent or opaque the given question is. The more transparent the money question is, the more conscious we are in our decision making. The more opaque it is, the easier it is to make less conservative decisions with our money. For example, how many times have you selected an on-demand movie that you would probably never have rented from the video store? The automatic billing catches up with you on the monthly invoice and, if you're like many, you're shocked by all the extra charges. But each month, with the remote in one hand and popcorn in the other, you do it again.

When an amount of money is extreme, either extremely small or extremely large, we tend to account for, and spend it, differently as well. For example, would you overpay for an item by 300%, 400%, or 600%? Ridiculous, you say? When the amount of money is relatively small, you might. Millions of Americans do it every day by raiding the hotel snack bar, for example. Isn't $8 a bit steep for a chocolate bar that costs just $1.50 in a convenience store down the street? How about when amounts are extremely large? Do you think people spend extremely large amounts frivolously? Well, of course they do. Think about a car purchase. People feel they need their options like heated seats and extra cup holders with independent suspension so that their decaf vanilla lattés with extra whipped cream don't spill. These *"while you're at it"* additions can pile thousands more dollars onto the price of the car. However, because they increase the monthly payments by only $20 or $30, people allow them to add up almost without thinking.

Car buyers are already spending a considerable amount of money—what's a little more? Registration, taxes, interest rate, delivery to lot, and insurance are some of the costs that are often overlooked. Many car buyers never actually see the money they're spending. The dollars they envision are merely represented by a number that's subtracted from their monthly budget, as opposed to actual dollars that are removed from their pockets and turned over to someone else. They say, *"Hey, I'm already spending $44,000. What*

*difference does another $2,000 or $3,000 or $4,000 make? What,
$775 for the sunroof? Sure, gotta have that."* A fancy new GPS navi-
gation system can run as much as $4,000, but buyers don't often per-
ceive it that way. They figure that if they're going to spend nearly
$44,000 on a car, how's an option that's less than 1/10 the price really
going to have a significant impact on the total price? When your ultimate destination is retirement, it may be cheaper to buy a map.

### The Proxy Perception

Using checks, credit cards, or room numbers at the hotel while
lounging about the pool are all ways that consumers buffer themselves from how much they're really spending. All these different
ways to pay make money more and more opaque to consumers and
provide perfect examples of **layering**. *Layering* is used as a money-
laundering term that refers to layers of separation from the place
where it was originally "earned."

Just as Las Vegas has learned that people will toss chips around
far more liberally than cash, the credit card industry knows very well
that people treat those little 3⅜ inch-by-2¼ inch plastic rectangles
very differently. Buyers are more apt to whip out their plastic, not just
because the fiscal impact of the purchase is muted, but also because
it's simply quicker and easier to pay that way. Think about retail trans-
actions in the 1970s: The cashier would ask, *"Cash or check?"* You
would then pull cash out of your pocket and turn it over to the cashier
who would go through an elaborate counting exercise in his head
because calculators weren't widely available, before giving you too little change—or too much change, in which case you would walk out of
the store as quickly as possible. You could also write a check, which
extended the checkout process by eons as you presented two forms of
I.D. and wrote down the amount of it in your check register. Writing
a check removed you from the hurt of seeing actual money leave your
possession, but at least you were keeping track of your balance.
Hmm, when is the last time most Americans balanced their checkbooks? Quaint little notion, isn't it?

Many Boomers may recall when cashiers counted change as they
handed it to you—but they counted back to the amount you had originally given them. In other words, accounting protocol dictated that if

you gave the cashier a $20 bill for an $11.19 purchase, she should count back to the original $20 amount by adding your change to the total purchase amount as follows, *"Here's the 81 cents, that's 12; 3 dollars, that's 15; and five makes 20."* That isn't what happens now, is it? Now the cashier will virtually never count your change at all. And if they do, they merely count the change out loud as they are handing it to you. *"Here's 5, 8, and 81."*

A swipe here and a swipe there and pretty soon you're talking real money.

Nowadays there's no waiting at retail and little appreciation of how much you're spending; you just swipe a credit or debit card and go. At the gas pump, at the fast food drive-thru, at the grocery store, we have become a *"Just Swipe It"* generation of spenders. And to further remove you from how much you're spending, a signature is seldom required for everyday purchases; in fact, the whole transaction is lightning quick, very convenient, and very opaque. Have you noticed how more and more checkout screens at retail stores are positioned in a way that the cashier can see what each product being scanned costs, but the customer cannot?

I was at a club-type store recently and noted that many of the departing customers were hurriedly scanning their receipts and checking prices as they pushed their carts toward the person at the door who matches their receipts with the goods in their carts. After all, this information was not available to them at the checkout station. And at this point, what happens when one of these consumers discovers that he was charged $3.79 for an item he is sure was supposed to cost $3.29? Is he going to get out of line, shuffle over to customer service, and spend the next 15 minutes getting his 50 cents, or is he going to push his cart on out to the car? And when there is a choice of receiving a receipt or not, many of us decline the offer of a receipt and arrive home with absolutely no idea how much lighter in the wallet we are. You have to wonder, if most consumers continue to decline receipts, will the default change? Will the customer be required to *ask* for the receipt in the future? Will gas pumps eliminate your option to print out a receipt? Or will we be told a receipt will be sent electronically? Years ago, the Apple Store started sending receipts to customers' e-mail accounts so that they could print them out if they wanted them, and there is a movement afoot to make "e-ceipts" a part of the retail landscape through an embedding of information in your credit cards. I am convinced that receiving a paper receipt is going to continue to be less and less common. At the gas station I frequent, the last question from the machine is *"Do you want a receipt?"* Yes, I know it will show up on my credit card anyway, but I hit "Yes," mainly because I don't want the option to go away—and my thinking is that if enough people keep hitting "No," the option will be eliminated.

Of course, there could be all sorts of fraud and privacy issues that would need to be overcome for e-ceipts to become common. And it is possible for *layering* technology to go haywire on its own without criminal intervention. For example, people who frequent toll roads often buy toll transponders and attach them on the dashboard of their cars so they don't have to stop and pay at the tollbooth each time they pass. We had a focus group participant who told us how the chip in her brother's transponder went haywire and kept overcharging him for multiple passes. The transponder account was set up so that the money came directly out of his checking account, and before he realized what had happened, her brother was $10,000 in debt. The woman's brother had to move in with her and hire a lawyer as the situation, still not resolved, has put the entire family in financial straits. This gentleman may have avoided this predicament if he'd paid at the tollbooth, or perhaps more importantly, paid closer attention to money flowing automatically out of his checking account. The layers that he put between himself and his money caused him to, in a way, fall asleep at the wheel.

Paying with a check. Paying with a credit card. Paying with those pinky-sized credit "cards" that dangle from your keychain. Paying by text message. Swiping your cell phone like a credit card. Who knows, someday we may simply think of a purchase and charge it. That might sound a little sci-fi, but there are now so many ways to pay because marketers are doing whatever they can to make it easier for customers to give in to impulse. For example, my wife and I were recently convinced to go on the first cruise in our lives—Vancouver to Alaska. Our friends, who are cruise veterans, assured us that this particular ship was the top of the line and that it would be an excellent vacation experience. They were right. There were daily excursions with exotic things to do, such as viewing glaciers, fishing salmon-filled rivers, bear watching, and more. All these adventures and thrills, of course, come at a significant extra cost. The cruise does a marvelous job of arranging and masking various combinations of these activities, so it is rather difficult to discern precisely how much any given outing costs. In fact, I was introduced to many new procedures and expenses as the lines blurred from one fun package to another. But, most intriguing is the $2,000 of upfront money called "ship credit." What a concept. You pay for ship credit in addition to the excursion packages, and in advance of the cruise, so that you've already parted with your money before you even begin. You can supposedly get money not spent back at the end of the cruise; however, the process is so complicated (standing in long lines, negotiating credit that will be returned to you) that it becomes easier to simply spend the ship credit that you originally purchased. That's the idea—to spend the money. Our friends, in fact, declared at one point, *"Well, we still have $150 left, we should stop by that jewelry store."* From a psychological standpoint, they had already recategorized that money as something other than their own.

As we've seen, *layering* can cause different degrees of separation from your money, and layers can be added between you and your cash by both proxy and by permission. The point is, the thicker the layers, the more opportunity there is for poor financial decisions. As we've discussed, *layering* can affect the way you make purchases and how you pay for labor. Table 2.1 starts with thin layers and shows how spending becomes more opaque as the mental layers get thicker.

**Table 2.1   Psychological Levels of Layering**

| Layer | Effect |
|---|---|
| Personal checks | When you write a check and make a notation in your account, the layer between you and your cash is fairly thin. |
| Credit cards with paper receipt signature required | When you sign for a purchase and get a receipt, you are at least aware of how much you just spent. |
| Credit cards with *electronic* signature required receipt | E-sign technology used at retailers, such as Target and Wal-Mart, speeds up the sales transaction, and you are less involved in the amount of money you spend. Many buyers just make a mark rather than taking the time to write a full signature. |

| Layer | Effect |
|---|---|
| Credit cards with no signature required and no immediate receipt | It's late at night, you're watching an infomercial, and you decide to make a purchase with your credit card over the phone to operators who are standing by. The next time you see that charge will most likely be on your credit card bill. |
| Pay with your cell phone | Mobile commerce is on the move. What started in Europe and Asia is rapidly expanding in the United States. Swipe your phone like a credit card, and you're on your way. |
| Chips | What happens in Vegas stays in Vegas—especially your money when casino chips are used as a proxy for cash and cause you to spend differently. |
| Approved hourly rate | When can a 15-minute phone call get prorated to a 1-hour fee? When you agree to the attorney's hourly rate. |
| Room key or *"having a tab"* | You're poolside or in the hotel bar and the waitress says, *"Would you like to charge that to your room?"* |
| Online credit information storage | Frequent online shoppers often store their credit and contact information online with the vendors they buy from. With just a few convenient clicks, you can fill your shopping carts with goodies and be on your way in a matter of minutes. The amount you spent could be a blur and a memory in no time. |
| Automatic pay | You agree to a 30-day free trial for a magazine subscription with the option to drop, but when you forget to act, you are charged for a year, and even more with automatic renewals. The default is designed to work against you. You join a wine club and permit the monthly fee to be pulled directly from your checking account for convenience. The problem is that wine shops are filled with wine that club members fail to pick up. |
| 12 months same as cash | If you borrow $1,000 on a 12-month, same-as-cash plan, you have to pay it back within 12 months to avoid interest. The problem is, if you borrow $1,000 and pay back only $950 of it in 12 months, you will be charged interest on the full $1,000. Guess what's making a comeback since the meltdown? *The classic layaway plan.* |
| Cruise ship credit | You are on a cruise and pay credit in advance, separating yourself from your money and mentally recategorizing it before you spend it. Expectation is to spend it by end of the cruise, even if you don't really need to. |
| Miniature radio frequency identifier | This device may sound sci-fi, but it does exist. A miniature radio frequency identifier, the size of a grain of rice, can be injected between a thumb and forefinger and with a gesture of the hand, pays for drinks at some clubs.[35] |

**Table 2.1   Psychological Levels of Layering (continued)**

| Layer | Effect |
| --- | --- |
| 401(k) debit card | Investors may think this sounds like a good idea, but who's the winner here? The problem is this money is supposed to be earmarked and invested for retirement. So, the question becomes, "Is this really a debit card or is it a retirement-draining card in hiding?" |

## VEGAS, BABY, VEGAS!

Las Vegas is one of the world's most popular playgrounds for grownups. The town is all bells and whistles and neon lights. Luxury hotel rooms, gourmet food, and the finest cocktails cost you little more than the lint in your pocket. Comedy acts and concerts raise the curtain around the clock—all of which is designed to get people and their money into the city's world famous casinos. When people are in the casinos feeling good, happy, and confident, the magic of Vegas really takes hold. From the lighting, to the carpet, to the ambient noise, Vegas casinos are designed to separate customers from their money legally and happily. A city like Las Vegas is not built on winners. Vegas is built on losers; losers who are happy enough losing that they keep coming back and keep losing. Basically, people become pleasurably mesmerized by the sensory overload that is Las Vegas and, eventually, nothing seems real—especially the money in their pockets. As Frank Sinatra reminded us years ago, *"Las Vegas is the only place I know where money really talks—it says, 'Goodbye.'"*[36]

To make it easier for people to lose more money, the casinos immediately devalue it. How? By pointing customers to the cashier's window upon arrival, where they promptly exchange their dollars for chips that they'll use at the gaming tables. Further devaluing the currency, dealers and croupiers and pit bosses call the red $5 chips "nickels" and the green $25 chips "quarters" and so on. What happens is that people toss down a chip and think to themselves, *"Hey, it's only a nickel,"* or *"What's a quarter good for these days anyway?"* Many housekeepers at Las Vegas hotels report that guests tip with chips instead of actual cash. Why? Tossing a "nickel" chip onto the bed is psychologically less painful than pulling out a $5 bill. It's even less painful than pulling out four $1 bills. When customers exchange their cash for thin rubber and plastic wafers, they divorce themselves from the full value of their cash; that action puts layers between their money and the value of that money. The casinos collect these colorful little proxies after their customers lose them; then the casinos turn them over again to the next person who approaches the cashier's window with his bankroll. If the walls of Vegas casinos could talk, they'd tell plenty of stories about gamblers who got caught up in the spirit of the place, treated their money in a way they would never treat it at home, and lost more than they could afford. So what happens in Vegas stays in Vegas, especially your money, if you don't set a budget before you convert your money into magical chips.

# The Retirementology Cash Challenge

If you're still unsure how the format of money makes a huge difference in the way you spend, take the **Retirementology Cash Challenge**. Put away your credit cards, debit cards, and even checkbooks, and try using only cash for a week. The amount of cash you realize you are spending will be eye-popping, but even so, you will most likely return to your credit or debit cards for the sake of convenience. If you must use plastic, which we all do, consider organizing your purchases in the following manner:

| Discretionary Spending | Nondiscretionary Spending |
|---|---|
| *Cash* | *Credit* |
| Restaurant dinners | Gasoline |
| Movies and sporting events | Groceries |
| Clothes, such as a $50 sweater | Car repairs |
| Gifts | Home repairs |
| Gourmet coffee | |
| Try to keep discretionary spending under 20% of your take-home pay. When you put away the credit cards and use cash for these items, you'll see how fast the spending adds up. | |

Let's take the Retirementology Cash Challenge one step further. What if I challenged you to spend no more than $100 on food for an entire week, and I gave you a $100 bill. If you accepted that challenge, my guess is that you would have an extremely good idea of how much you had spent and had left at the end of, say, Day 4. Further, you would have a very clear idea of whether a purchase of a $7 cheeseburger made sense about now. But many people are so distanced from their funds—by electronic statements and layered forms of payment—that they really aren't sure how much they're spending, how much they owe, and how much they have left. Their funds show up automatically and electronically in their accounts. Many of their bills are paid the same way. The balance ebbs and flows without the consumer having a clear understanding of whether flow is exceeding ebb—or by how much. One of the best steps people can take is to simply dig in and get a very clear picture of all this. Do you know precisely how much money you owe right now—credit cards, mortgage, and so on? Do you know what your average monthly spending was last year? Do you know how much of this was discretionary? Do you know what your average monthly net income was last year?

# Improve Your Retirementology IQ

People make plenty of errors when it comes to setting a financial plan for retirement. You can improve your Retirementology IQ by recognizing the following common mistakes:

**Mistake #1: Are you spending too much?** The first error of anyone planning for retirement or just budgeting between paychecks is, of course, spending too much. Simple first-grade math should tell anyone that overspending will only get you in trouble. Although the Greatest Generation didn't have access to all the sophisticated financial instruments we have today, they did exhibit one thing very well— they lived within their means. That's a lesson that's as valid today as it was during the Great Depression.

Before you consider purchasing a home theater system, new car, or remodeling your home again, think about how much that luxury could potentially cost your retirement. Chances are your lifelong spending has a greater impact on how you retire than you are aware. In Figure 2.1, let's take a look at some spending boom luxury purchases and what they are really costing your retirement. Is that luxury really a necessity?

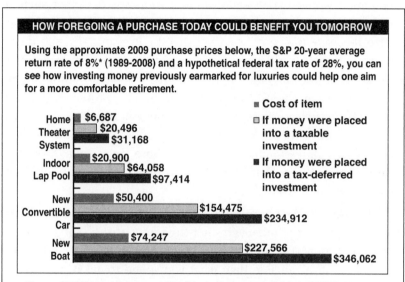

**HOW FOREGOING A PURCHASE TODAY COULD BENEFIT YOU TOMORROW**

Using the approximate 2009 purchase prices below, the S&P 20-year average return rate of 8%* (1989-2008) and a hypothetical federal tax rate of 28%, you can see how investing money previously earmarked for luxuries could help one aim for a more comfortable retirement.

■ Cost of item
□ If money were placed into a taxable investment
■ If money were placed into a tax-deferred investment

Home Theater System: $6,687 / $20,496 / $31,168
Indoor Lap Pool: $20,900 / $64,058 / $97,414
New Convertible Car: $50,400 / $154,475 / $234,912
New Boat: $74,247 / $227,566 / $346,062

*Source: S&P Historical Returns. www2.standardandpoors.com/spf/xls/index/MONTHLY.xls

This hypothetical example assumes the purchase of certain items versus investment of the purchase price in either a taxable or tax-deferred vehicle, based on an average rate of return over a 20-year period. It assumes no subsequent investment or withdrawals. This illustration is not intended to reflect the past or future performance of any product and does not reflect any fees and charges associated with investment products. If reflected, the results shown would be reduced.

Lower maximum tax rates on capital gains and dividends would make the investment return of the taxable investment more favorable, thereby reducing the difference in performance between the accounts shown. Please consider your personal investment horizon and income tax brackets, both current and anticipated, when making an investment decision, as these may further impact the results.

The investment totals in this illustration show the 20-year accumulated sum before any withdrawals. In the event that a lump-sum withdrawal was made, taxes would not reduce the 20-year total of the taxable investment, but would reduce the 20-year total of the tax-deferred investments. Withdrawals may also incur fees, penalties, state and federal taxes, and the total available would be less than the cumulative figures shown in the chart above. Tax-deferred totals would be reduced as follows: Home Theatre System—$22,441; Indoor Lap Pool—$70,138; New Convertible—$169,137; New Boat—$249,165. The assumed tax rate is hypothetical and may or may not reflect an individual's actual tax rate.

The items mentioned in this hypothetical example include: home theater with Bose Lifestyle 28 Series III Home Theater System and Panasonic TH 65" plasma widescreen TV, 2008 Endless Pool Standard System, 2009 335i Convertible, and 2008 FORMULA 24.

**Figure 2.1    To Buy or Not to Buy**

**Mistake #2: Are you setting a budget?** Much of the past six decades have seen the American economy grow. As a result, many people's incomes have grown and their lifestyles have gotten more and more lavish: It's hard to believe a member of the Greatest Generation would have treated himself to a "spa day," but such an indulgence is fairly common now. Setting a budget allows you to prioritize the importance of what you need and want. If a spa day is important, what would have to be cut? Too often, this trade-off is excused as everything is put onto a credit card and a minimum payment is made at the end of every month. The problems that can emerge from such a lack of discipline are legion, but they can be easily avoided with a simple budget. A weekly budget, a monthly budget, even a yearly budget allows you to see where your money would go before it goes there; that allows you to decide just how important some things are to you.

**Mistake #3: Are you keeping high-interest credit card balances?** Credit is not money. It's not the same as cash being dropped into your account. Credit is to be used only if it can get something for you that is more valuable than what you spend to get it. Otherwise, using credit becomes nothing more than an unnecessary expense that can cost you the retirement you're after. Some people will set aside cash in a low-interest account for an "emergency" or "rainy day" fund and that's fine. But not if that account is earning a fraction of the interest that you're paying on your high credit balance. A high credit balance is a parasite on all other savings and investments; it's imperative that you eliminate that balance as soon as possible, starting with the balance upon which you're paying the highest interest...then build up the cash reserve. Start with your highest interest balances and pay those off; then move to your next highest interest balance, and so on.

**Mistake #4: Are you keeping low insurance deductibles?** It may seem attractive to you to have a low deductible for your car and home insurance. If you have an accident or a fire, for instance, you only have to pay a small amount of money toward getting your situation rectified. The price you pay for such a low deductible is, however, a much higher premium. That means more money coming out of your monthly budget, money that can be doing much more good going into your retirement accounts and earning compound interest.

Push your deductibles as high as you can, and you'll have better control of your money.

**Mistake #5: Are you keeping a high balance in your checking account?** If you keep a great deal of money in your checking account, the size of any given check you write looks a lot smaller. If you have $5,400 in a checking account, a $532 check looks rather large. In fact, it changes the first number on the balance, which keeps your attention. But if you are holding, say $100,000, in your checking account, that check barely puts a dent in your account, and that makes it easier to keep writing checks and to lose accountability for what you are spending. Effective October 3, 2008, the Emergency Economic Stabilization Act of 2008 increased the Federal Deposit Insurance Corporation's (FDIC) coverage limit to $250,000 per depositor. This limit will revert to $100,000 on January 1, 2014. In my opinion, that is probably a lot more money than a smart saver should ever have in a checking or savings account.

# Enjoy the Sushi...Just Hold the Gold Dust

A comfortable retirement is available to just about any American who shows just a little self control. Sure, you're going to spend money—there is no free lunch...or dinner, for that matter—but after you pay your taxes, you do have control over how much you spend. The fact is that many experts cite controlling spending as the single most important ingredient to building wealth. In their classic book, *The Millionaire Next Door*, Drs. Thomas Stanley and William Danko describe a person who controls his spending as *"playing good defense."* Indeed, the bankruptcy courts are full of people who have won or earned a great deal of money, but their taste for living the high life is what drives them into financial trouble.

## Curb Spending

Do you really need that triple mocha latté with sprinkles for $3.50 every morning? On a larger scale, what about the heated seats with the *Magic Knuckles* massage system on every seat in your new car? Sure, this luxury adds *only* an extra $50 onto an already big $900 monthly car payment, so it doesn't feel like it's really hurting your budget…especially when you're getting a massage as you roll down the road. But a little here and a little there can add up to real money and cost thousands of unnecessary dollars in the long run. That's money that could be growing and helping you accumulate even more for retirement. If you really do need to spend, spend your dollars wisely.

**Mental budgeting.** My father taught me the game of chess as a child, and at one point in my life, I was quite an enthusiast. I purchased one of those chess computers from Radio Shack that beat me with infuriating consistency. The problem, of course, was that the computer could sort through the labyrinth of combinations much more quickly and clearly than I could. But I found that the one way I could actually win, though rare, was to reduce the complexity of the puzzle. I would set a game plan in place specifically attempting to trade as many evenly valued pieces whenever I could—a knight for a bishop, a pawn for a pawn, a queen for a queen. In this way, I was reducing the number of decisions available. Extrapolating this, if I could reduce the game to a point where we each had a king and three pawns remaining, my odds of winning were greatly improved. Similarly, I believe you can implement this type of strategy from *mental accounting* that can be a very positive and soothing technique for managing your expenses. For example,

- The $437 per month received from my pension at my old employer is my dining out fund.
- This year's bonus is our "new car" fund.
- The dividend from the oil and gas stock funds our long-term care insurance.

*Use mental budgeting to your advantage.* Setting a budget for a week or a month is a great way to curb spending. Setting a top-end price that you're willing to pay for a big-ticket item is also a way to keep yourself from spending money that could better be put toward retirement. Mental budgeting can help you determine different needs and time horizons for different pools of money. It may be to your advantage to budget with a purpose, with a firm timeframe and an acknowledgment that your total budget and wealth plan is composed of different parts that have a purpose and are uniquely suited to your overall retirement objectives.

| Needs on the Horizon (5 Years) | Needs Beyond the Horizon (20 years) |
|---|---|
| Kids' College Tuition | Retirement |
| New Car | Long-Term Care |
| Landscaping for House | Grandchildren's College Fund |

## Use Financial Automation

In 1934, an R.H Macy & CO. executive and New York Fed director named Beardsley Ruml developed a plan whereby the U.S. Treasury would remove a certain percentage of money from every American's paycheck to pay that person's taxes.[37] The government got the money before the worker did and the age of automatic withholding was born. IRS aside, you can use the power of automation for saving and investing, as it simplifies the process for building a retirement nest egg, encourages disciplines such as dollar cost averaging, and keeps the focus on a long-term retirement perspective. It should be noted that dollar cost averaging does not guarantee a profit or protect against loss in a declining market, and it involves continuous investing regardless of fluctuating price levels. So, you should really consider your ability to continue investing through periods of fluctuating market conditions. However, by automating your contributions, you can better assess how much money you have to spend on day-to-day items. Remember, a retirement nest egg is like a bar of soap; the more you touch it, the smaller it gets. Don't peek and keep it out of reach.

## Regularly Increase Your Contribution Rate

The automatic payroll deduction structure of 401(k) accounts can help investors stick to a more disciplined retirement plan. Professor Richard Thaler of the University of Chicago, and Professor Shlomo Benartzi of UCLA, took this strategy one step further. They created a program called Save More Tomorrow (SMarT), which is currently being adopted by some 401(k) providers. Under this program, workers agree to boost their 401(k) contributions automatically by two to three percentage points with each annual raise. During a four-year test of the SMarT Plan at a mid-sized corporation, participants' average contribution rates jumped from 3.5% of their pretax pay to 11.6%.[38]

With the passage of the Pension Protection Act (PPA) of 2006, companies began using automation to increase participation in their qualified plans. Instead of just promoting the plan and waiting for participants to sign up, many employers have begun to automatically enroll employees. Research shows when automatic enrollment is implemented, participation can reach 95%.[39] Although company automation is a powerful tool and has helped jumpstart plan participation for many workers who may have otherwise procrastinated, the PPA also opened the door for automated processes such as autodefault and auto-advice, which can both lead to problems. When auto-enrolling workers, many companies set the default rate too low, for example 3%. Although something is better than nothing, a low contribution rate can prevent participants from earning company matches, which means you could be losing out on free money if you don't adjust your contribution rate. The automatic advice that many companies offer is likely in the form of hard-to-follow sales literature, often presented by a human resources employee, rather than a financial professional. If you choose to do nothing, auto-enrollment could lead to a low default rate and an auto investment selection that may not be right for you. For example, in recent years, target date funds have been the default du jour for 401(k) plans, and unfortunately, they were down as much as 40% last year,[40] so they haven't fared any better than most other investments. It's no secret that 401(k)s, in general, took a beating during the market meltdown, but they are still one of the most effective tools for building your nest egg over time— especially if you work with an adviser and take full advantage of what your company has to offer.

Consider the following five factors with your retirement account.

| Factor | Problem | Solution |
|---|---|---|
| 1. **Participation** | Fifty percent don't participate.[41] | Participate and max out contributions, or at least contribute enough to take advantage of the company match. |
| 2. **Portability** | Forty-six percent of people cash out when they change jobs and suffer heavy tax consequences.[42] There's also a 10% penalty if the person cashing out is not yet age 59½. | Work with a financial professional to roll over assets into a retirement vehicle, such as an IRA. |
| 3. **Loans** | Yes, with "heavy" tax consequences.[43] | Establish an emergency cash fund—avoid borrowing from your 401(k). |
| 4. **Investments** | Acting as own chief investment officer. Eighty-four percent of employers say their employees are confused about fund options.[44] | Diversify your portfolio based on your risk tolerance. |
| 5. **Education** | Only 37% of employers offer employees access to financial advice regarding their 401(k) plans, and 53% of employers say their employees do not know how much they will need for retirement.[45] | Ask your employer for all available information. Then work with an adviser to get the most out of your individual plan. |

# RETIREMENT ISN'T A SINGULAR EVENT—SPENDING IN YOUR 20S, 30S, AND 70S HAS AN IMPACT ON YOUR RETIREMENT. FURTHER, RETIREMENT ISN'T ISOLATED—WHAT YOU SPEND ON A VACATION OR CAR MAY IMPACT YOUR RETIREMENT LATER.

# Endnotes

1   Hopkins, Jerry, Anthony Bourdain, and Michael Freeman, <u>Extreme Cuisine: The Weird & Wonderful Foods That People Eat</u>, 2009.

2   Gold Bulletin, "Gold leaf tops $1,000 sushi roll," April 17, 2008.

3   Cooking Resources, "Cooking With Edible Metals Like Gold, Silver," October 29, 2009.

4   Gold Bulletin, "Gold leaf tops $1,000 sushi roll," April 17, 2008.

5   *Business Week*, "After the Housing Boom," April 11, 2005.

6   Credit Card News, "Ditching credit cards right move for some," September 22, 2008.

7   NPR, "Credit Card Companies Raise Minimum Payments," November 4, 2005.

8   *The New York Times*, "Economy Fitful, Americans Start to Pay As They Go," February 5, 2008.

9   *The New York Times*, "Given a Shovel, Americans Dig Deeper Into Debt," July 20, 2008.

10  *The New York Times*, "Given a Shovel, Americans Dig Deeper Into Debt," July 20, 2008.

11  *USA Today,* "Obama team makes it official: Budget deficit hits record. By a lot," October 16, 2009.

12  *The American*, "Debt Be Not Proud: The Sorry Tale of America's Out-of-Control Spending," September 7, 2009.

13  Brillig, U.S. National Debt Clock, as of January 14, 2010.

14  Market Watch, "Financial fears grow," March 20, 2009.

15  Market Watch, "Financial fears grow," March 20, 2009.

16  Market Watch, "Financial fears grow," March 20, 2009.

17  Yahoo! Finance, Starbucks Corp. (SBUX): Historical Prices, Jan. 1, 2007–Dec. 31, 2007.

18  Navellier Growth, "As Starbucks (SBUX) Stumbles, Green Mountain Coffee Roasters (GMCR) Shines," April 16, 2009.

19  Broadcast Engineering, "Big-screen LCD TV sales grow in 2007, research firm says," February 19, 2008.

20  Recreational Boating & Fishing Foundation, Boating & Fishing Facts, 2006 Recreational Boating Statistical Abstract, 2007.

21  *The New York Times*, "Hummer's Decline Puts Dealers at Risk," March 31, 2009.

22  *The New York Times*, "MTV's 'Super Sweet 16' Gives a Sour Pleasure," April 26, 2006.

23  iStock Analyst, "Retail Survey Report: Cache Stores, Chili's, Chuck E. Cheese," July 23, 2008.

24  What It Costs, "Top Ten Most Expensive Parties Ever Thrown," 2009.

25  Answers.com, "Jackie Mason," 2009.

26  MetLife, "The American Dream has been revised not reversed, pragmatism is replacing consumerism as the bar stops rising/buyer's remorse sets in, according to third annual MetLife study," March 9, 2009.

27  *The New York Times*, "Given a Shovel, Americans Dig Deeper Into Debt," July 20, 2008.

28  *The New York Times*, "Given a Shovel, Americans Dig Deeper Into Debt," July 20, 2008.

29  *Fare Magazine*, "Consumers Cut Back on Coffee Spending," January 30, 2009.

30  *Ventura County Star*, "Stores out to tempt TV buyers this week," January 25, 2009.

31  *The New York Times*, "Hummer's Decline Puts Dealers at Risk," March 31, 2009.

32  *The New York Times*, "Hummer's Decline Puts Dealers at Risk," March 31, 2009.

33  *San Diego Union-Tribune*, "Parents scale back luxuries for children," June 14, 2009.

34  Pew Research Center Publications, "Luxury or Necessity? The Public Makes a U-Turn," April 23, 2009.

35  CreditCards.com, "Implantable credit card RFID chips: convenient, but creepy," August 5, 2009.

36  Notable Quotes, Quotes on Las Vegas, from *The Joker Is Wild*, 1957.

37  Encyclopedia definition of Ruml, Beardsley, 2009.

38  Thaler, Richard, and Shlomo Benartzi, "Save More Tomorrow: Using Behavioral Economics to Increase Employee Saving," November 2000.

39  WebCPA, "Automatic 401(k) Enrollment Is Not for Everyone," October 27, 2009.

40  *The New York Times*, "Target-Date Funds: Seven Questions to Ask Before Jumping In," June 29, 2009.

41  *Pensions & Investments*, "Special Report: The Looming Retirement Disaster," April 18, 2005.

42  Hewitt, "Hewitt Study Shows Nearly Half of U.S. Employees Cash Out Their 401(k) Accounts When Leaving Their Jobs," October 28, 2009.

43  *USA Today*, "401(k) loans come with caveats," October 11, 2007.

44  Watson Wyatt, "The Defined Contribution Plans of Fortune 100 Companies: 2008 Plan Year," Research Report – December 2009.

45  Watson Wyatt, "The Defined Contribution Plans of Fortune 100 Companies: 2008 Plan Year," Research Report – December 2009.

# 3

# The NoZone

**ZONED OUT:** [zohnd out]

Irrationally believing that one can tune out retirement-related decisions because he is not yet "in the zone." *Because he did not plan on retiring for 15 more years, Andy zoned out on his retirement planning.*

Imagine it's the championship game with 10 seconds left on the clock and your team is down by 2 points. The quarterback is taking one last snap to move the ball a little closer to the goal line to set up a winning field goal. Your team is in the *red zone*, which in football signifies that a team is within 20 yards of the goal line, and where statistics show your team scores a high percentage of the time. But what if...the quarterback takes a bad snap and fumbles; the other team recovers the ball, takes possession, and holds on for the win. Shock. Dismay. Disappointment. Game over.

For the past few years, several financial firms have borrowed the red zone metaphor from football, referring to the five years before and the five years after someone's retirement as the red zone, and popularizing the notion that the few years remaining prior to retirement are somehow the most critical to a successful retirement. Then along came the worst economic crisis since the Great Depression, and millions of Americans' retirement plans were sacked for a loss just short of the goal line—in this case, just as they were preparing to enter retirement. What has become clear is that solving the retirement conundrum requires attention much earlier than a handful of years prior to retirement...and will certainly continue well into retirement. In June of 2004, the Dow Jones Industrial Average, an index which is a price-weighted average of 30 actively traded blue-chip stocks that generally are the leaders in their industry, was over 10,000.[1] During the next three years, it climbed above the 14,000 point.[2] Numbers were dizzying. Investors were jubilant. Untold heights were ahead. *Risk* was nothing more than a board game we played when we were kids. And then...the meltdown. What's happened in recent years has destroyed or delayed an entire lifetime's worth of retirement plans. Now millions of Boomers may be seeing red, but there is no zone in sight.

Waiting until you're in the so-called retirement red zone before you plan for retirement leaves you susceptible to bad luck or events over which you have no control. That's because proper retirement planning doesn't start five years before you finish work and end five years into retirement. Retirement is not an event, a compartment, or a zone. Retirement is a monetary process that takes a lifetime of preparation that is predicated by a lifetime of behavior when it comes to your spending, borrowing, saving, and investing. If you're breathing and able to earn money, you're in the zone *right now*. Those who wait until they get into the red zone to start preparing for retirement put themselves in a position where an unforeseeable event—a bad snap and a fumble, or a financial meltdown and flight to low-risk investments—can cost them the retirement they were expecting. The recent financial meltdown is a perfect example of an unforeseeable event, and it cost retirement investors untold millions of dollars...many of them were Boomers who lost great sums of money at a time when they could least afford it: just before or just after they entered retirement.

Planning for retirement and retirement income is more like a 50-year project than a 10-year project. In fact, the real red zone may well be the first 5 years of an investor's earning years. Out-of-pocket expenses and obligations are fewer for a young person, and the money that's invested then has more opportunity to grow thanks to the power of compounding. I discussed in preceding chapters how a person can invest a relatively small sum in her 20s and watch it grow to a much bigger sum than someone who starts investing in her 50s and puts in much more principal. Just think of how much can change in a short amount of time when you have a market downturn. Consumer confidence is one thing that went from high to low. The Conference Board's monthly Consumer Confidence Survey is conducted every month by research company TNS Global. TNS surveys 5,000 U.S. households and asks five questions that determine the respondents'

- Appraisal of current business conditions
- Expectations regarding business conditions six months hence
- Appraisal of the current employment conditions
- Expectations regarding employment conditions six months hence
- Expectations regarding their total family income six months hence

For each question, the three responses from which to choose are POSITIVE, NEGATIVE, and NEUTRAL. The response proportions to each question are seasonally adjusted and, for each of the five questions, the POSITIVE figure is divided by the sum of the POSITIVE and NEGATIVE to yield a proportion, which they call a "relative" value. For each question, the average relative for the calendar year 1985 (the year it equaled 100)[3] is then used as a benchmark to yield the index value for that question.[4]

But the Consumer Confidence numbers weren't the only ones that dropped precipitously from 2007 to 2008. The Dow Jones Industrial Average also fell in a hurry during that time.

### Then...pre-meltdown

- In November 2007, the Consumer Confidence Survey checked in at a rather robust score of 87.3.[5]
- On October 8, 2007, the Dow was at 14,043.[6]

### Now...post-meltdown

- In October 2008, the Consumer Confidence Survey had dropped to 38%, the most pessimistic number in more than 25 years.[7] In fact, 62% of American adults now believe that today's children will not be better off than their parents.[8]

- On September 15, 2008, the stock market would begin a three-week slide that would see the Dow lose 2,937 points, or 26% of its value.[9]

# The Retirement Brain Game

**Regret and pride**—People avoid actions that create *regret* and seek actions that cause *pride*. *Regret* is emotional pain. *Pride* is emotional joy. Is this causing us to buy high and sell low? Research indicates that two of the most troublesome emotions that plague investors are pride and *regret*.

**Myopic loss aversion**—One type of event in particular has overwhelming, disproportional impact on investors—loss. As we discussed in the Introduction, research shows that, on average, before people would be willing to risk loss, they would need to see their gains reach at least 2.25 times the potential loss. This is what led Dr. Richard Thaler to conclude that losses hurt 2.25 times more than gains satisfy. When most investors experience loss, they spend the rest of their lives in fear of it. Fear of loss dominates their thinking—fear of missing out, fear of looking stupid, fear of not winning—all dimensions of loss. Wanting to avoid loss is understandable, especially when it comes to something as important as your retirement plan. However, it doesn't mean that avoiding loss should be the primary objective of your investment strategy.

**Herding**—In behavioral finance the concept of *herding* is all about chasing trends. Day in and day out, investors purchase a stock simply because the company is recommended by an analyst or because media coverage is elevated and pronounced. The idea being, *"Everyone else is buying those shares, so why shouldn't I?"* Prior to the meltdown you should have been asking, *"Is today's hot trend a worthy gamble for my nest egg?"* Since the meltdown, you may be asking, *"Is the mattress the only place safe enough for what's left of my money?"* Why shouldn't you be asking yourself these questions? Everyone else is. A related concept is the Odd Lot Theory, which is a technical analysis theory that's based on the assumption that the small individual investor is always wrong. So when odd lot sales are up, it's because small individual investors are selling as a herd—and that could mean a good time to buy.

## Thrill, Euphoria, and Other Things That Make You Sell at a Loss

"**Regrets**, *I've had a few*," as the song goes. When we miss a bus or a train or a plane by minutes, we're much more upset than when we miss it by an hour. When we're way behind, we have a way of giving into the fact that we're not going to achieve what we were hoping to achieve and we make other plans; there's no sting in the loss. There was a study conducted on the pain and anguish of Olympic silver medalists compared to bronze medalists. In a nutshell, at the end of a close race, a silver medalist always looked disappointed, whereas the bronze medalist looked proud that he would be on the medal stand at all. Why is that? How can people be happier about coming in third than second? Perhaps it's a feeling of achievement; just achieving a place on the medal stand is more gratifying than coming up *just* short of achieving a gold medal.

In reality, a loss is a loss. But when just missing a connection or falling just short of a goal, the *means* can be more important than the end result. I have a friend whose wife was sitting in a restaurant when she realized her necklace had come off. She quietly looked around the table for it before calmly announcing to her dinner companions that the necklace was gone. After hearing a description of the necklace, another woman at the table said, "*I saw one just like it in the rest room not 5 minutes ago.*" Overcome by the possibility of being so close to retrieving her lost necklace, she ran into the ladies' room to look for it, but the necklace was nowhere to be found, and the feeling of *regret* overcame her. *Regret* is a powerful emotion, but one that doesn't always allow us to look at the past with objectivity. My wife's friend was no closer to retrieving her necklace from the ladies' room than she was when she first discovered it missing.

Regret often clouds our retirement planning. Behavioral finance expert Meir Statman said, "*Emotions are useful, even when they sting.... But sometimes emotions mislead us into stupid behavior. We feel the pain of regret when we find, in hindsight, that our portfolios would have been overflowing if only we had sold all the stocks in 2007. The pain of regret is especially searing when we bear responsibility for the decision not to sell our stocks in 2007.*"[10] Many people were buying stocks at the end of the most recent bull market and started selling them as their value went down. Unfortunately, after a market downturn, many people fall into this pattern of buying high and selling low. Our fear, our confidence, and our emotions convince us to take irrational chances with our investments. We often pull money out of the market when the market goes down and wait until it gets back to its highs to buy again. We repeat the same pattern of buying high and selling low. If you're doing this, you're not alone.

### Loss: A Cautionary Tale

What **myopic loss aversion** means is that we have become so short-sighted, so fearful of loss, so concerned with losing our money, that we often make no decision, or make the wrong decision—either of which may prove costly. For example, suppose your child just entered college and the $10,000 bill for his tuition is due. You can either sell Stock A, for which you paid $20,000 and is now worth $10,000. Or you can sell some of Stock B for which you paid $20,000 and is now worth $30,000. *Which will you sell?* Research indicates that investors will most often choose the latter—despite that the tax deduction would make selling the loser even more attractive.[11] Why? Quite simply, Americans hate to lose! And how does this impact our expectations for investment returns? Today things are different. Now, people are scared. And how is this fear manifesting itself? It is causing investors to place disproportionate amounts of their portfolios into overly conservative investments. People have also stashed away a tremendous amount of cash in savings bank accounts and in the form of CDs and money markets. In short, most of us no longer want to destroy the market, we want to make sure that the market does not destroy us. We don't care as much about gains as we do about avoiding further loss. Several years ago, it was about the fear of not participating. Today, it is about the fear of losing.

From the euphoria of a bull market, to the despondency of a bear market, investors often follow a cycle of market emotions that all too often results in buying high and selling low (see Figure 3.1).

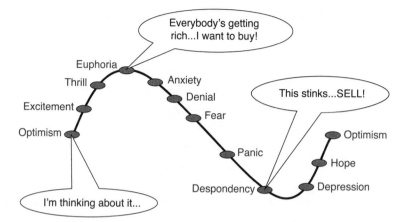

Source: Westcore Funds/Denver Investment Advisors LLC, 1998 (emotional roller-coaster visual only)

**Figure 3.1   The Cycle of Emotions**

ComPsych, one of the world's largest providers of employee assistance programs, reported in 2008 that 92% of polled workers said financial worries were keeping them up at night.[12] The 19th Annual Retirement Confidence Survey by the Employee Benefit Research Institute in April 2009 revealed that the percentage of workers who have lost confidence about having enough money for a comfortable retirement continued a two-year decline with only 20% saying they're very confident. And that makes sense. The Institute revealed that 36% of workers 55 and older say the total value of their savings and investments (excluding the value of their home equity and any defined benefit plan they have) is less than $25,000. Whether that low number is a result of poor planning or the meltdown, clearly these future retirees have reason to worry. The report went on to say that 89% of Americans plan to change the way they manage their personal finances, and 94% say the meltdown will have a long-term effect on the way they manage their investments...not surprisingly, a vast majority of them (81%) indicate they'll pull back and *"play it safer with investments."*

There is a science to taking control of your retirement planning. It starts with understanding what you want to do, what gets in the way of your doing it, and what you can do to avoid those pitfalls. Consider a fundamental financial strategy called dollar cost averaging, which many investors practice without even realizing it when they make

regular contributions to their 401(k), for example, and keep contributing no matter what the market's doing. I'd like to reiterate that
dollar cost averaging does not guarantee a profit or protect against
loss in a declining market, and it involves continuous investing
regardless of fluctuating price levels. Investors should really consider
their ability to continue investing through periods of fluctuating market conditions. So how could such a machine-like approach to investing have anything to do with investor psychology? Well, it's *"not
rational,"* reported Meir Statman when speaking about automated
investing, *"but it is pretty smart."*[13] Basically, engaging in a program
of dollar cost averaging takes your mind away from the decision of
what is the best time to invest because your mind has already made
the decision *when* to invest. If you set up a program to invest on the
first Monday of every month and the market goes down immediately
after your first investment, you don't have to worry because that only
means that your second investment will allow you to buy even more
shares. According to Statman, *"the strict 'first Monday' rule removes
responsibility, mitigating further the pain of regret."*[14]

According to research conducted by the University of Minnesota,
people who are stuck in traffic feel better about the progress they're
making if they're moving at a consistent 5 miles per hour than those
having to constantly stop and go, and actually moving faster at an
overall average of 10 miles per hour.[15] The loss of a couple minutes
here and couple minutes there while sitting still in traffic, it turns out,
was so frustrating that the people surveyed didn't appreciate the
progress they were actually making. No matter what people are trying
to do, anything that appears to slow down their progress toward that
end is seen as a loss and is avoided at every opportunity. But what
happens when you follow the driver in front of you without paying
attention to the road signs?

### Money in Emotion

If you were to get into the head of a lemming, who was hurling off
a cliff to his death like all the other lemmings, the little rodent might
be thinking, *"Why wouldn't I jump off a cliff? Everyone else is doing
it!"* What causes a stampede to start? A single piece of bad news

can devastate a stock's or segment's value just as a single piece of good news can result in its value going up. The late 1990s and early this century brought us the "Dot Bomb." Every day it seemed there was another 23-year-old kid who started a company with "dot-com" at the end of it who was suddenly an instant millionaire. *Whatever.com, wake-up-late.com, latest-greatest-idea.com*—wheeling-and-dealing professional investors, as well as individuals planning for their own retirement, gobbled up shares of these companies and asked for more. The market cap of these companies shot through the roof until a turn of events brought down the house of cards. Boom! The **herding** mentality reversed itself, and everyone sold shares, many for less than they'd paid because so many bought into the companies when they were heavily overvalued.

The Dot Bomb was just one of many bubbles in the annals of human beings hoping they could sell what they had to the greater fool and secure riches for themselves. Tulips, of all things, were one of the great early sources of wealth and the creation of a bubble. In 1624, about 60 years after rulers of the Ottoman Empire were first enchanted by the vibrant colors that could only be found in tulips, a Dutchman in Amsterdam turned down a great deal of money for a single tulip bulb. For the next dozen years, tulip bulb prices shot up—a farmhouse was purchased for just three bulbs—as auctions attracted more and more people who were more and more willing to purchase the flowers. Fortunately, however, the Dutch stock market did not deal in tulips, so the only people hurt were those who were left holding them when the price went down.[16]

One of the most compelling arguments against *herding* is that it can create just such a bubble, where the investment is pushed up to unreasonable levels based on emotional reasons rather than a logical estimation of worth. Take the nationwide housing bubble, for example. As home prices skyrocketed, investors poured in and snapped up properties to the tune of billions of dollars. In my opinion, even as housing prices continued to climb well above reasonable valuation levels, people piled in at a near frenzied pace. When the housing market cooled, however, those same investors fled in droves, collapsing the bubble. A *herding* mentality helped create the bubble, and that same *herding* mentality caused its eventual collapse, fueling one of the most ravenous foreclosure markets this country has ever seen.

And who got caught in the crosshairs? Everyday people, that's who. Ordinary folks who were just trying to make a better life for their families suddenly found themselves upside down on their mortgages. And as the economy continued to shrink and shed jobs, many of those same people found themselves simply unable to pay the mortgage and put food on the table at the same time. Or worse yet, in their exuberance to get in on the hot housing market, they accepted ballooning adjustable mortgages that quickly grew beyond the constraints of the family budget. Innumerable other scenarios undoubtedly played a role, but the end result was undeniable: The bubble had burst, and a *herding* stampede had played a preeminent role.

# Improve Your Retirementology IQ

These are scary times for an investor and for a retiree. But this is not the first time we've had an unnerving investment landscape. Understanding some retirement basics is a good start. Rather than following the herd, consider following these fundamental steps.

### *Understand Your Objectives and Assess Your Risk Tolerance*

You must understand where you are in life, where you want to go with your financial future, and how much risk you are willing to take, or should take, to get you there. There are two key points to understanding your objectives: the anticipated cost of the objective and the timeframe you have to meet your objective. The absence of one of these points of reference makes it impractical to plan financially to meet your objective or to assign an appropriate level of risk to your investment decisions.

Traditionally, long-term investors have opted for greater risk on the belief that it would, over the right period of time, produce greater rewards. For example, historical data suggested that equity investments tend to outperform fixed income investments over time. However, the day-to-day volatility of the stock market generally makes equity investments a risky bet for short-term needs. In the context of retirement planning, equity investments provide long-term growth potential and a hedge against inflation but have greater volatility. Therefore, having equities as part of your retirement portfolio may be the right move. On the other hand, if you have immediate income needs or plan to draw income from your portfolio in the near future, investments that guarantee the return of your principal may be smarter, even though the actual rates of return on these investments may be less attractive.

It is also vital to weigh the importance of meeting your objectives within a given timeframe when considering risk. For example, if you would "like" to retire in five or six years, you may find that the financial resources you have available would require you to generate an aggressive rate of return on your investments to reach your objective. By accepting a high-level risk to meet your objectives, you may reach your goal, but you would have to balance that with the reality that poor performance or even losses on your investments may keep you from reaching your objective and may delay your retirement. In other words, if the due date of your objective is flexible, taking an additional risk for the chance of reaching it sooner may be an option. On the other hand, if your son or daughter is going to college in five years, taking on additional risk to meet the objective may not be all that responsible because the objective—your son's or daughter's college years—isn't flexible.

You should also consider the level of risk that is required to meet the objective and only take on as much risk as required to meet your objective. For example, if we assume an investor had accumulated $2 million for retirement and his annual income needed in retirement was $50,000, his required rate of return on his investments would be 2.5%, assuming his objective is to preserve his principal balance. He could meet his income objective with very little risk. There is no need for him to take on additional risk to meet his objectives. Of course, not everyone is fortunate enough to be able to invest in low-risk investments and adequately meet income needs in retirement.

For example, if we assume this individual had invested $500,000, he would need a rate of return of 10% each year to meet his retirement objectives. A 10% rate of return would require a substantially higher level of risk and, most likely, greater volatility. Your risk tolerance and the amount of risk you are willing to take when it comes to your retirement nest egg are important considerations when determining how much you need to invest and when you will retire. So, the less risk you can take to meet your objectives, the more comfortable you may be in meeting them. Understanding your own personal objectives and risk tolerance will help you overcome the desire to herd with the masses.

## Set Long-Term Financial Goals

The achievement of any goal requires a plan. A goal without a plan is a wish. *Where do you see yourself in 10, 20, or 30 years?* An investment decision based on what happened during the fall of 2008 or the bursting of the dot.com bubble a few years earlier would be a very short-sighted way to invest. But many people based all their decisions on these events and turned what they had left into cash. The tragedy for many is that we've had a bull market since March of 2009, and many people have not participated. Hersh Shefrin wrote in his book *Beyond Greed and Fear* that short-term needs battle with long-term needs in any plan or budget. The short-term needs are right in front of people, almost screaming at them. Long-term needs are way off on the horizon; a faint voice that can barely be heard. The key to following a long-term retirement plan is to always pay heed to the voice that's off in the distance because it will get closer and it will get louder and that will happen much more quickly than you think. If you start planning for retirement now, you'll be glad later that you did. If you don't start planning for retirement now, you'll wish that you had. It's that simple. Regardless of age, if you haven't started accumulating money for retirement, you should start immediately, and put the potential power of compound interest to work for you. Further, if you haven't done a basic analysis of how much you may need for retirement, you may want to put it on your to-do list.

Consider the following: If we assume that a person graduates from college at 23 and plans to retire at age 65, he has 42 years of full-time employment to prepare for retirement. If we assume that the average person lives to age 85, he will spend 20 years in retirement. In other words, you have approximately 2.35 years of income for every year of retirement. Given the difficulty many people have in just making ends meet throughout life as they save for their first house, raise their children, and eventually send them off to college, it's not surprising that people often put off planning for retirement until they're "older." The problem is that when people feel they're in a position to plan for retirement, they're shocked at how much they need to accumulate to fund the retirement they desire. If you want to get a better idea of when you will be in a position to retire and what it will cost, you need to start planning as soon as you can get a plan in place. Plans help you stick to commitments and avoid regret, as well as the fear of loss.

### Decide on an Asset Allocation Strategy

The road to your financial security is full of obstacles that you need to negotiate. Your asset allocation strategy can help you through these obstacles by helping you reduce the impact of market and economic volatility. An asset allocation strategy is synonymous with the old adage *"don't put all of your eggs in one basket."* As the last few years have taught us, markets and the overall economy can be volatile and hard to predict. Investing all your assets in one place or in one type of investment vehicle is closer to gambling than it is to prudent investing. By spreading your assets across multiple asset classes, you reduce the overall risk associated with just one asset class. An appropriate asset allocation also takes into consideration your risk tolerance, your financial resources, and your timeframe. The way you view or frame your portfolio can also help you diversify it. View your portfolio in the broad sense as a whole, rather than in a narrow sense, in pieces and parts. And view your portfolio as a long-term tool, rather than a day-to-day investment. In other words, *"aggregation can reduce aggravation"* when it comes to managing your portfolio.

## *Periodically Evaluate Your Plan and Strategy*

Over time, it's easy to get off course as your financial journey unfolds. You should periodically evaluate your direction to see if changes are needed. You may want to rebalance your portfolio from time to time to make sure that it represents the risk and diversification you desire. It's very unlikely that your financial resources and financial burdens and responsibilities will follow a nice, neat linear path to retirement. There will be windfalls and there will be setbacks. For this reason, it is important to reevaluate your financial plan on no less than an annual basis. Try to pick a day, like New Year's Day or your birthday or April 15th, to reassess your financial plan and see what changes should be made. Sitting down and doing a budget and creating a financial plan are good ideas, but you will find that any plan and any budget will become less and less applicable as time goes on. Your risk tolerance will change, your appropriate asset allocation will change, and your financial resources will change. Therefore, your plan will have to change accordingly if you want to meet your long-term goals and objectives.

## *Develop a Financial Plan*

When you know the goal for your financial future, you need a road map to get there. Your financial plan provides the direction needed for this journey. Most people tend to avoid the "B" word at all costs. By the "B" word, I'm referring to a budget. Every financial plan starts with a budget, because before you can accumulate any money for retirement, you have to figure out where the money is going to come from. As I previously mentioned, finding enough money to make ends meet is difficult for most people, but you have to make retirement part of your budget. Setting money aside on a monthly basis is a start, but try to take advantage of retirement plans through your employer or by putting money into an IRA. There are limitations and penalties for removing money from these retirement vehicles prior to age 59½,[17] hopefully making it a little more likely you'll leave the money there until retirement. Use a financial planning calculator available on the Web or sit down with a financial planner to see where reallocating $25 a month will get you when you reach age

65. You probably won't be thrilled with the result, but you'll have a frame of reference from which to start. You'll begin to see how much of a difference an additional $25 or $50 or $200 will have on your retirement, and you'll begin to get a better understanding of what it will take for you to meet your financial goals at retirement.

Your plan will change over time as your financial situation changes. If you get a raise at work, consider increasing your retirement plan contributions. One good way to increase retirement contributions automatically is to make them a percentage of your salary instead of a dollar amount. Then, every time you get a raise, you increase your contribution. When retirement plan contributions are part of your monthly budget, you'll find that you can get by on what's left, and your retirement plan will start to take shape.

No one can tell what the future holds—who could've predicted the DJIA would drop from 14,000 to 6,600 in a little over a year? But a plan gives you an idea of how best to prepare for the future. Be honest about your goals. If you want to have access to $2 million cash on the day you retire, a house that's paid off, a winter house on the beach, and a golf cart to drive to the store from your beach house, put together a plan that you believe will take you there. Remember, there is no one-size-fits-all solution; you have to develop a plan and select the investments that work best for you.

**RETIREMENT ISN'T A ZONE; IT'S A CONTINUUM—
ONE YOU NEED TO START THINKING ABOUT
MUCH SOONER THAN FIVE YEARS OUT.**

# Endnotes

1  Yahoo! Finance, Dow Jones Industrial Average (^DJI): Historical Prices, Jan. 1, 2004–Dec. 31, 2004.

2  Yahoo! Finance, Dow Jones Industrial Average (^DJI): Historical Prices, Jan. 1, 2007–Dec. 31, 2007.

3  The Conference Board, "The Conference Board Consumer Confidence Index® Declines in October," October 27, 2009.

4  The Conference Board, "Consumer Confidence Survey® Methodology," 2009.

5   The Conference Board, "The Conference Board Consumer Confidence Index Declines," November 27, 2007.

6   Yahoo! Finance, Dow Jones Industrial Average (^DJI): Historical Prices, Oct. 1, 2007–Oct. 31, 2007.

7   The Conference Board, "The Conference Board Consumer Confidence Index™ Plummets to an All-Time Low," October 28, 2008.

8   Rasmussen Reports, "62% Say Today's Children Will Not Be Better Off Than Their Parents," October 3, 2009.

9   Yahoo! Finance, Dow Jones Industrial Average (^DJI): Historical Prices, Sep. 15–Oct. 31, 2008.

10  *The Wall Street Journal*, "The Mistakes We Make and Why We Make Them," August 24, 2009.

11  Nofsinger, John R., <u>Investment Madness</u>, Prentice Hall, 2001.

12  AARP, "Why Money Worries Are Keeping Us Up at Night," November 10, 2008.

13  *The Wall Street Journal*, "The Mistakes We Make and Why We Make Them," August 24, 2009.

14  *The Wall Street Journal*, "The Mistakes We Make and Why We Make Them," August 24, 2009.

15  The Wilson Quarterly, "The Traffic Guru," Summer 2008.

16  *Business Week*, "When the Tulip Bubble Burst," April 24, 2000.

17  About.com, Tax Planning: U.S., "Tax Penalty for Early Distribution of Retirement Funds," November 3, 2008.

# 4

## House Money

> **EQUIMORTIS:** [ek-wi-*mawr*-tis]
>
> Dangerous condition that can occur from counting on one's home appreciation for retirement money. *Only after the tenth foreclosure hit Colleen and Larry's neighborhood did they realize that they were in a later stage of equimortis.*

Remember Auntie Em's house from *The Wizard of Oz*? You can picture it swirling in the sky and that music is playing in your head right now, right? Sure, it could fly through the air, rid the world of a wicked witch, and cause a young girl and her dog to incur the wrath of the witch's evil sister. But other than that, it was a pretty Spartan structure...one storey and cozy cellar, and it likely did not possess granite countertops, stainless steel appliances, or a steam shower. But it was home for Dorothy. It was the place she counted on sleeping every night, year in and year out, until she was an adult; and even then, it was the place she envisioned coming back to for the rest of Auntie Em's life to visit. Yep, in spite of the fact that it lacked the sort of niceties that many of us take for granted today, it was home to Dorothy Gale, and she insisted that there was no place like it. But how would she feel if Auntie Em's house had a mortgage that was $200K more than its market value? Or if, because of being deeply underwater and unable to either sell the house or afford the monthly payments, Auntie Em might well have to move out in a few months?

Or if Dorothy had to explain to all her friends why she would no longer be in the classroom next year? In today's housing environment, Dorothy just might have been safer on the yellow brick road.

## How Did Owning a Home Become So Important?

Homeownership at the beginning of the 20th century was little more than a pipe dream for many Americans, conditioned by generations of renting with roots planted in both Europe and America. "*You must pay the rent,*" was the familiar cry of evil landlords in urban areas of America. Lower-income citizens began dreaming of homeownership as a means of getting out from under the thumb of those ruthless landlords who could easily turn a rental building into a rathole, while exacting the monthly rent, raising the rent, or simply throwing a family out on the street for any number of reasons, even if they paid the rent.

So what turned the poor man's pipe dream into the American Dream? In a word: war. Many indicators point to the post-World War I generation as the first generation grabbing their piece of the pie. With the rich economic climate of the Roaring 20s, dreams became realities for many families. And although the Great Depression killed many dreams, it did not kill the dreamers, as the emotional attachment to homes or the idea of owning a home became even stronger. Homeownership again flowered after World War II when the GI Bill sent many servicemen to college and trade school, and VA loans made it possible for them to purchase their own homes miles away from where they worked—a major socioeconomic development of the post-war era.

Homeownership gained momentum through the decades and became rooted in the public consciousness during the '50s, '60s, and '70s. But by the 1980s and certainly in the 1990s, the emotional attachment to owning a home underwent a dramatic transformation. Almost overnight, homes became viewed as more than simply a place to hang our hats and rest our heads. They became investment vehicles. Suddenly, the shortcut to retirement was as easy as following

Dorothy's yellow brick road. Just buy a property, or maybe a couple of properties, and ride the appreciation highway. The emotional attachment to our homes had a new tenant: A fiscal attachment, which may have caused many homeowners to overborrow, overspend, and overestimate the value of their homes.

## House Rules: ATMs on Steroids

It used to be that an American's investment in a home was as solid as the home's foundation: No matter what, a homeowner could be counted on to make his monthly mortgage payments. That's why mortgage-backed securities were considered such a solid investment. The bonds that were backed by the payments of mortgage holders over the lives of the mortgage threw off consistent income simply because mortgage holders would forego just about anything to stay current with payments on their #1 asset, their homes. Over the years, homes have become more than just a roof over a homeowner's head. They've grown, they've become more luxurious, and they've even become a central part of a homeowner's retirement planning from a financial standpoint.

Consider the average home a generation or two ago as opposed to now. In the 1970s, the average American home was about 1,500 square feet; today it's more than 2,400 square feet.[1]

The home has always been a centerpiece of American life, but in recent years, the home and houses in general have come to dominate the focus of millions of families within a wider and wider socioeconomic range. CNBC produced a two-hour special program titled *House of Cards*, which aired in January 2009 and featured interviews with many people who purchased homes and then pulled cash out in refinancing. A typical story would involve a buyer purchasing a home for, say $500,000, and then refinancing when it had appreciated to, say $700,000, perhaps as little as a couple of years later. In that show, one buyer was quoted as saying, *"We bought the house and had $100,000 in equity before we even got in the front door."* A remarkably common theme in these scenarios, along with how many of them had exaggerated their income levels to qualify for the loans in the first place,[2] was how they seemed to use that money after refinancing. Usually, at least a portion of it was put right back into the home—a new swimming pool, kitchen, patio, bathroom, or new landscaping. The home was seen as the golden goose. It was the ticket to a better life, it was new cars, college education, vacations, and so on—and it was expected to be the ticket to a better retirement.[3]

# America's Housing Boom

From 1997–2005, overall homeownership grew in all geographic regions and for all age groups, racial groups, and income groups.[4] The housing price boom cited in *The Economist* not only dwarfed all previous housing booms, but also it was larger than the stock market bubble of the late '90s.[5]

- Real home prices for the United States as a whole increased 85% between 1997 and the peak of the housing bubble in 2006. Nationally, median home value rose from $78,500 in 1990 to $185,200 in 2006, a 136% increase.[6] From 1995 to 2001, home values increased 68% in Boston, 71% in Denver, and a full 100% in San Francisco.[7]

- As a result of the federal government "streamlining" the regulatory requirements in the mid 1990s for loans, "...*federal bank regulators required banks to make bad loans based on nonexistent credit standards.*"[8] "*Under increasing pressure from the Clinton Administration to expand mortgage loans among low and moderate income people...the government-subsidized corporation may run into trouble in an economic downturn, prompting a government rescue similar to that of the savings and loan industry in the 1980's.*"[9]

- Cow pastures were converted into $500,000 homes. Mortgage originators were pushing credit out the front door to citizens— and pushing shaky mortgages out the back door to banks to securitize and bundle with other such loans.

- Daniel Sadek's Quick Loan Funding was originating so many loans in southern California that he pulled in a reported $37 million in one year.[10]

- Nonstandard loans (less than 5% down) jumped from 9% in 1991 to 29% by 2007.[11] Freddie Mac and Fannie Mae kept capital markets liquid enough so that banks and mortgage originators could award loans to consumers. These two government-sponsored enterprises (GSEs) provided a market for securitized subprime mortgages. Other companies, such as Bear Stearns and Lehman Brothers, also got into the business of buying subprime mortgage-backed bonds.[12]

- Everything having to do with houses and home improvement was also booming. For example, Home Depot, a penny stock in 1985, went from $50 per share at the beginning of 1997 to $79 at the end of 1999.[13] Over the past decade, it's hovered between $20 and $45. Lowe's, the other big name in home improvement superstores, was also a penny stock in the mid-1980s that saw its stock rise with the housing boom.[14]

# It's Not Just a House; It's a Celebrity

In December 1994, the vision of a broadcast manager and weekend architect named Ken Lowe came to life when HGTV took advantage of a massive cable expansion and became available in 6.5 million homes.[15] The network's prime-time lineup of programming was almost entirely original, and its advent would introduce an entirely new kind of programming. And for the next 15 years, HGTV and other networks would feature a multitude of television reality shows starring house flippers, extreme-makeover specialists, and do-it-yourselfers, programming that consistently grew in popularity. Shows with some dimension of homeownership for both vocation and recreation became a national obsession, as the entire country seemed to become advocates for the home improvement industry. Sure, PBS's iconic *This Old House* had been around for years and had attracted a dedicated niche of viewers every week. But HGTV wasn't just about restoring failing and historic homes; it gave viewers an insight into projects, large and small, for houses that were perfectly fine. The network's hosts quickly became celebrities, and their influence could be felt nationwide as the network showed viewers how to update and, yes, increase the value of their homes.

A January 3, 2009, *The Wall Street Journal* article titled "Blame Television for the Bubble," stated, *"You couldn't watch these shows without concluding you must be an idiot and a loser if you lived in a house you could actually afford."*

### America's Housing Bust

*"Let's hope we are all wealthy and retired by the time this house of cards falters."*

—Excerpt from an S&P employee email, December 15, 2006[16]

Nationwide, housing values started to fall in the autumn of 2007.[17] To the surprise of no one with the benefit of hindsight, the Dow Jones Industrial Average peaked then as well at 14,164 on October 9, 2007.[18] As Robert Shiller, Yale professor, economist, and long-time real estate expert predicted, so much of America's wealth—or at least the wealth effect, the feeling that we were wealthy—was tied to the rising values of our homes.[19] When people's homes stopped appreciating in value, a homeowner could no longer draw money from it...and that homeowner certainly couldn't draw money from a bank account that never had any money in it. In a shockingly brief period—perhaps six months—I believe homes went from being many of Americans' most significant retirement planning tool, and largest recipient of love and attention (save for their immediate families), to being their greatest financial liability. The "lock box" in which they took such pleasure in knowing that they possessed $100,000, $200,000, or $500,000 of wealth was suddenly underwater by the same amount.

# From "A" List to "D" List

The home was an investment that was supposed to move gradually and nearly always north, and suddenly it was behaving like pork bellies during a swine flu outbreak. It wasn't merely a "negative adjustment" to their portfolios and psyches; it was, in many cases, a complete reversal.

- In the third quarter of 2009, there was a record number of foreclosures; it was the worst three months of all time.[20]

- The national median home price of single family homes sold during the first quarter of 2009 fell 13.8% to $169,000 year over year, and 6.2% compared with the last quarter of 2008, according to the National Association of Realtors (NAR). That was the largest year-over-year decline in the 30-year history of the report.[21] To use an example of an extremely overbuilt market, the average home value in Phoenix in 2006 was $227,000, and as of this writing, the average home value in Phoenix is $104,000, which is a drop of 54%.[22]

- The National Delinquency Survey conducted by the Mortgage Bankers Association recently reported the largest quarter-over-quarter increase in foreclosure since it began keeping records in 1972.[23] A report from the Center for Responsible Lending, a consumer advocacy group based in Durham, NC, says that 2009 foreclosures alone will cause an estimated 69.5 million homes to suffer price declines averaging $7,200 per home. The loss in property value could total $500 billion, and the balky economy, along with continually rising unemployment numbers, portend that the property value losses may continue to grow. The Center's report relied on forecasts from Credit Suisse, which said late last year that about 9 million homes would probably go into foreclosure in 2009 to 2012.[24]

- Daniel Sadek: Quick Loan Funding was just a vehicle for Sadek to start a film production house he called Redline Productions. During a promo for his first film, *Redline*, his million-dollar Ferrari Enzo was totaled, a perfect metaphor for the industry that allowed him to buy the car in the first place.[25]

- Home Depot stock dropped from the $79 high in December of 1999[26] to just $22 by December of 2008.[27] Lowe's stock also took a significant hit dropping 78% in early 2009 from a $68 high in 2006.[28] As homes lost value, home improvement became an afterthought. To encourage homeowners to continue to renovate their homes, the City of Denver gave out free construction permits to homeowners and licensed contractors making qualified home improvements or repairs to existing one- and two-family dwellings. To spice up appeal, the city called the promotion a *Home Renovation Bonanza*.

- To boost stagnant ratings, new HGTV programs have been introduced to better suit today's downsized audience. A sample of new shows includes *For Rent*, an old concept gaining new appreciation, *The Unsellables*, where homeowners get help selling homes that have been on the market for months, and *The $250,000 Challenge*, where cash-desperate contestants try to get out of the hole they dug with their overpriced homes.[29]

In general, the bloom may be off the rose in terms of Americans' attitude toward homeownership. A survey from the National Foundation for Credit Counseling garnered these results.[30]

- Forty-nine percent of the respondents said that the American dream of homeownership was no longer a realistic way to build wealth.
- Thirty-two percent said that they didn't think they would ever be able to own one.
- Forty-two percent of those who once had owned a home said that they didn't think they would ever be able to buy another.
- Of those who still owned a home, 31% said that they didn't think they would be able to afford to upgrade or buy a second home.

## The Retirement Brain Game

**Wealth effect**—It's often said that "perception is everything," and the behavior of countless homeowners during the housing boom went a long way in adding credence to this philosophy. Encouraged by rapidly rising home values, homeowners became victims of the *wealth effect*, perceiving and believing that they were wealthier than they actually were and unfortunately spending accordingly.

**House money effect**—When gamblers experience big wins, they are willing to take more risks and often refer to this as "house money." Treating money differently, and in many cases recklessly, when a gain or profit is realized, is known as the *house money effect*. During the housing boom, millions of Americans used the equity in their homes like house money for home improvements, vacations, new cars, or even more houses.[31] And now, for those who rode the perpetual rise of home appreciation, many bets are off.

### On the House

Although there were myriad culprits behind the credit crunch, Boomer behavior such as the **wealth effect** and **house money effect** played a prominent role. Robert Shiller's book *Irrational Exuberance*, published in 2000, detailed the trouble that awaited us all when the impending Nasdaq bubble burst. He argued that it was the artificial rise in home values, not the tech stock boom, that was creating the dangerous wealth effect. And that was in spite of the fact that demand was decreasing in important markets such as Silicon Valley.[32] As tech stock values were pushed higher by a bubble, the *wealth effect* took hold and had people feeling wealthier than they were, and the same thing happened with the housing bubble that followed. Worse, the *house money effect* began to show itself as an offshoot of the *wealth effect*, leading to riskier and more careless spending of what homeowners viewed as their windfall money.

Their windfalls inspired homeowners to keep updating and making their houses more valuable—or so they thought. But it was *house money*, money their investment had earned that they were playing with when they took out home equity loans and poured that money back into their houses. This quintessential example of how the *house money effect* had such a strong hold on the American population was that we spent approximately $262 billion during the first half of 2005 on home improvements.[33] Much of what was spent was money that was realized as a result of a home equity loan, made possible by the home's value increasing. Pulling even more money out of their homes made many Americans go from house poor to house destitute.

### From Ego Boost to Ego Bust

Intertwined with the fiscal rewards of home value appreciation was the added benefit of making all homeowners look like geniuses—smart in their financial acumen as well as their domestic tastes. Yes, many a couple undoubtedly sat poolside on their newly constructed patios and toasted each other with glasses of reserve chardonnay. *"How many other couples are this smart, honey? Make a pretty good team, don't we? What with my house hunting and negotiation skills and your eye for redecorating, we've made ourselves a cool $200K in* *just the last three years! You know, I've been watching that 'Flip and Retire Young' show. I think we could actually teach them a thing or two.*" Unlike any paper wealth that the tech bubble might have produced, the housing boom gave millions of Americans a daily reminder of just how smart they were. They woke up daily to the palace they had no business owning and got to revel in its benefits—the neighborhood, the space, the views, the granite counter tops, the Jacuzzi, and, of course, the status. Yes, Americans grew overconfident in many ways these last ten years, but none more than in their views of their own real estate expertise and in the ability of their homes to essentially cure all fiscal ills through unending, consistent, jaw-dropping appreciation.

And make no mistake, now that the money's gone, much more than just the pocket books of Americans have been damaged—many an ego has also been badly bruised. It's no stretch to say that couples are no longer proudly toasting each other's real estate genius, but instead licking their wounds as they join the ranks of America's growing house poor.

House poor is, of course, the phenomenon that many first-time homebuyers historically go through when they purchase their first house, after curbing spending to save for a down payment that depletes their accounts to make the biggest purchase of their young lives. In a traditional market that's not all bad, though it's always smart to have other diversified investments. Of course, the perception of being house poor disappeared when house values were shooting up in value. For the millions behaving differently with their windfall money, the buzz of home appreciation and the equity they thought they could bank on was considered "on the house."

Let's look at a hypothetical tale of two neighbors. *Savvy Sam* treated his house like a home rather than a piggybank, and today, while he's down, he's not out.

**Savvy Sam:** I bought my house for $500,000. I watched enthusiastically as it appreciated to $750,000 and was sick to my stomach as it fell 50% to $350,000. Fortunately, I aggressively paid down my mortgage and now owe only $250,000...no mistake about it, this downturn hurts, but I will survive.

In the book *The Book Casino Managers Fear the Most! 777*, gambling expert Marvin Karlins established that people behave much more loosely with house money. They place bigger bets, they place more unrealistic bets...and then when they lose it, they try to get it back by continuing the betting patterns that caused them to lose their house money in the first place.

**Naïve Ned:** I bought the exact same model at the exact same time as Sam. Unfortunately, I refinanced five times, as the price appreciated, taking out cash and financing $8,000 in closing costs each time. Today, I owe $650,000 on my $375,000 house...and by the way, I'm in foreclosure.

The *house money effect* likely influenced many homeowners to become flippers, people who buy a house and then turn around and sell it (presumably) for a profit in a short time. This kind of buyer has always been a part of the home buying market, but the sudden allure of large profits being made during the housing bubble drew in the inexperienced and naïve. Mistakes that many house flippers made, and continue to make, are neglecting the sorts of big-ticket items that can come up as problems during a home inspection. A roof that needs to be replaced can easily cost $10,000. An old furnace and water heater can be just as much. Siding or windows that are subpar need to be updated, and landscaping is an expensive proposition that can't be overlooked if a person is looking to sell a house.

## PROFILE: The Flip That Flopped

Lance Becker, a second-generation real estate broker, who I interviewed in June of 2009, has a lifetime of understanding about the real estate business. Many of the stories he tells about people who've made real estate mistakes feature a person who sees a great remodel or makeover on television and decides to do the same sort of thing. What many people don't understand or appreciate is that renovations involve lots of money and lots of hard work. That doesn't always come across on television, where the point is to entertain the viewer.

*"There are a lot more flips that flop than make money,"* said Becker. *"People have bought into the TV shows and many have been burned, especially after the market tanked, but even before,"*

he added. According to Becker, one flip that went bad took place in Park Hill, a charming old neighborhood on the east end of Denver. There are a number of wonderful, old shops and new restaurants in the area, as well as The Denver Museum of Nature and Science and the Park Hill Golf Course, from which you can take in the Denver skyline and the breathtaking Rocky Mountains. The neighborhood is populated with old "Denver Four Square" and Tudor houses, most of which are still in great shape a century after they were originally built. As Denver's population has increased over the past 25 years, so has the desire for many people to buy a home in one of Denver's old neighborhoods. The prospect of living in such a manageable city, only blocks from downtown and a few miles from the mountains, is a big draw. That's why the houses in Park Hill have undergone so many upgrades and today command a hefty price.

Becker recalls a gentleman who got into the house flipping business and set his sites on Park Hill. He purchased a 1910 Tudor and promptly went about making first-class updates to the main floor. Walls came down so that people in the living room and dining room could easily converse with people in the kitchen, where granite countertops and the latest in stainless steel appliances made this the epitome of a cook's kitchen. He coupled the redesign with updated wood floors and other niceties, and the first-time house flipper couldn't wait to bring potential buyers in and let the bidding begin.

As expected, people were impressed when they stepped into the house. When they went upstairs to the bedrooms, however, they saw something that was completely inconsistent. Four bedrooms, each about the size of a queen-sized bed, and one common bathroom made up the floor. The floor plan was a relic of a time gone by…a time gone way by. When the house was built, the upstairs was probably considered roomy. In the 1950s, a full bathroom upstairs might have been considered a luxury. But today, a house in a "granite countertop neighborhood" is not complete without a substantial master suite. Potential buyers saw the upstairs and were completely turned off. The few who were still interested would have to consider all the costs to be incurred updating the upstairs and building new kids' bedrooms somewhere else in the house or even adding on; that led to a series of lowball offers.

After having the house on the market for nine months, the inexperienced flipper had to take in renters to meet the mortgage payments. When the upkeep and mortgage proved too taxing on his time and budget, he wound up selling the lovely Tudor at a huge loss, and he is out of the business.

Becker concluded, *"The real estate market has been crazy over the last several years. Amateurs, like this flopper, have jumped in and limped out; and the expectations of homebuyers have been over the top."* Easy money and unrealistic appraisals conspired to attract people into the real estate market, people who would otherwise have spent the past number of years working and saving and investing to build their wealth or put together a down payment for a house down the road. The prospect of quick profits for house flippers drew people to the business who had no business getting involved. As for overly zealous home buyers, it seemingly became the norm to live in an expensive house in which they had no equity. *"The good thing about the bubble bursting is that we can get some sanity back into this business,"* says Becker.

## Got a Pulse? Get a Loan!

Federal policies initiated to promote homeownership for more people introduced the law of unintended consequences into the American Dream. The genesis of this mess is the Community Reinvestment Act (CRA) of 1977, which passed the 95th Congress and was designed in part to encourage increased homeownership within lower income neighborhoods via access to loans from deposit-taking financial institutions.

One of the developments of the Act was an end to the practice of "redlining," or disqualifying someone for a home loan in certain ZIP codes. The term was coined by community activists who noted that the failure of banks to make loans in some low-income neighborhoods was so geographically distinct that it was easy to draw a red line on a map to delineate the practices.[34] The CRA was proposed by Senator William Proxmire of Wisconsin for the purpose of eliminating the practices of redlining and "credit exportation," where money is taken from a low-income community via deposits and lent to borrowers outside of the community.[35]

In spite of the bill's laudable goals, it did have its share of opponents, who called it *"thinly-disguised credit allocation"* that *"would represent a foot in the door toward the mandatory allocation of credit."*[36] Following the Fair Housing Act of 1968 and the Equal Credit Opportunity Act of 1975, among others, the CRA laid the groundwork for a practice that some people would call "predatory lending"—others would more bluntly call it lending money to people who had no business borrowing.

How predatory and irresponsible were the lending standards that helped create the credit crunch? Consider this excerpt from an article written in November 2008 by Michael Lewis,[37] author of *Liar's Poker*, regarding a loan company in California. *"(It was) moving money out the door as fast as it could, few questions asked, in loans built to self-destruct. (The company) specialized in asking homeowners with bad credit and no proof of income to put no money down and defer interest payments for as long as possible. In Bakersfield, California, a Mexican strawberry picker with an income of $14,000 and no English (sic) was lent every penny he needed to buy a house for $720,000."*[38] Time-tested practices of home selling, such as having the buyer make a 20% down payment, became passé. Mortgages for 100% of the asking price were suddenly common and the sellers— often because they were home flippers trying to make a quick sale— started paying the closing costs. Southern California mortgage originator Bill Dallas, chairman of OwnIt Mortgage, was interviewed for the *House of Cards* special and touched on the fact that if his company started asking for documentation for a loan, potential homebuyers would walk out the door and go to one of his competitors. The only way for OwnIt to stay in business was to follow a truly flawed business model…and simply stave off the company's own demise.

As outlined in Table 4.1, such products as no-money-down "liar loans," in which applicants simply stated their income without verification, as well as "Alt-A loans," in which borrowers generally had limited documentation and credit scores too low to qualify for what is classified as a prime (A-paper) loan, were promoted by banks and lending institutions across the country, many of them with adjustable rates that reset at much higher rates after a year or two.[39] Stretch loans, in which people would pay more than 50% of their income on the mortgage, were promoted by lenders, as were the colorfully named NINJA (no income, no job, and no assets) loans,[40] and with more buyers coming into the market, homeownership jumped to record levels.

Of course, very few of these new buyers were employing the time-tested 30-year, fixed rate mortgage that had proven solid for generations.

**Table 4.1   Nightmares on Elm Street**

| Type of Loan | Description |
| --- | --- |
| No-Money-Down Liar Loans | Applicants simply stated their income without verification. |
| Alt-A Loans | Adjustable rates that reset at much higher rates after a year or two. |
| Stretch Loans | People would pay more than 50% of their income on the mortgage. |
| NINJA | No Income, No Job, and No Assets. |
| Piggy Back Loans | Home financing option in which a property is purchased using more than one mortgage from two or more lenders. |
| Low Initial Fixed Rate Mortgages | Mortgages that initially have very low fixed rates and then quickly convert to adjustable rate mortgages. |
| Option ARMs | Interest-only, adjustable-rate mortgage (ARM), which allows the homeowner to pay just the interest (not principal) during an initial period. |
| Payment Option Loans | Mortgages in which the homeowner can pay a variable amount, but any interest not paid is added to the principal. |

## Opaque Adjustable-Rate Mortgages

For many Americans, a regular monthly mortgage payment is at the center of the family budget. When you make a down payment, pay a closing cost, and establish a monthly payment, you can see it clearly. It is transparent. You understand what you owe and know how it fits into your budget, and you can see what progress you are making toward completion of your mortgage. Most important, you can plan for it. For the millions of Americans who opted for an adjustable-rate mortgage (ARM), or an interest-only loan, however, budgeting is much more opaque. Option ARMs, which represent over \$230 billion in outstanding mortgages,[41] have triggers that reset to a new interest rate based on either a set timeframe or when debt exceeds some cap above the loan's value (see Table 4.2). And with interest-only loans, which allow a homebuyer to qualify for a more expensive house, the homebuyer puts very little money down and only pays on the interest owed for a number of years, which can affect financial planning in a number of ways. For example, homeowners with these loans may believe they can stay in their home a few years and then sell it at a profit as the home appreciates. However, as we've seen recently, by delaying payments that build equity, the chances for being "upside down" in one's mortgage increase.[42] For instance, during the meltdown, we've seen many homeowners who now owe more on their house than it's worth and may be waiting much longer than expected for their homes to appreciate.

The bulk of outstanding option ARMs—a product no longer available to homebuyers—were issued between 2004 and 2007, during the height of the housing boom. Monthly payments on these mortgages are due to reset to a higher lending rate between 2009 and 2012.[43] Analysts put the current default rate on option ARMs at 35%, and because they were most popular in states with the largest home price declines, many borrowers owe 40% more than their homes' current values. As more and more homes came back to banks as vacant structures instead of performing loans, the banks stopped lending money to people. Americans with ARMs that were about to reset could no longer refinance and needed to find money to pay their new higher monthly mortgages. That got them into trouble. A house is a home—that's the story you have to take from this episode.

**Table 4.2  Transparent Versus Opaque**

| Transparent | Opaque | Takeaway |
|---|---|---|
| *Monthly Mortgage* | *Adjustable-Rate Mortgages & Interest-Only Loans* | *Know What You Have* |
| Clear; current; consistent; budget friendly. Upfront down payment, closing costs, and lending fees. | ARMs and interest-only loans were promoted (and sometimes combined)[44] in a cloudy, future-oriented and complicated way. Minimizing out-of-pocket expenses, rolling the costs into other loan provisions, or delaying payments that build your equity (as with interest-only loans) can lead to bad surprises down the road. | Know the intimate terms—both for today and throughout the duration of the loan—before signing any contract. |

In an environment like the one we're in now, it's important to remember that decisions must be based in rational terms, especially when they involve something as important as retirement planning. As respected financial reporter Jason Zweig has written, *"Our investing brains often drive us to do things that make no logical sense—but make perfect emotional sense."*[45]

# Improve Your Retirementology IQ

If you start thinking about something that's already as emotional as a home like it's an investment, rather than shelter, you may do things that make no logical sense. When it comes to being smart with your house, the difference between boom and bust may well be doing your homework.

## Check Out Refinancing Options

In response to the credit crunch, there's been plenty of manipulation of interest rates. Today we have some historically low rates and plenty of homeowners who could do well to lower their monthly payments. The best thing any homeowner can do right now—especially a homeowner who has a solid credit history—is to call the company that presently owns his mortgage and see what sort of rates are available. There are a number of simple-to-use tools on the Internet to help you calculate whether refinancing is advantageous for your situation. One rule of thumb states that you may want to look at refinancing when rates are one percentage point lower than your rate, but many factors need to be considered.

Before you even consider refinancing, make sure your credit is in good standing. With the housing ride we've just had, good credit is more crucial than ever. The best way to maintain and improve your score is to know your score and know how scoring is compiled.[46]

- Payment history: 35%
- Amounts owed: 30%
- Length of credit history: 15%
- Types of credit used: 10%
- New credit: 10%

Refinancing is even available for homeowners who are underwater on their mortgages, as the president's foreclosure prevention program went into effect on October 21, 2009. The basic goals of the $75 billion program are to help homeowners refinance into loans with lower rates with more affordable monthly payments and encourage lenders to restructure mortgages to affordable levels.[47] You may be able to set up a program with your mortgage lender to make bi-weekly payments instead of monthly payments.

### Overpay Your Mortgage Each Month

If you plan to stay in your home, consider kicking in an extra $100 or so to your mortgage's principal payment; you can save tens of thousands of dollars. What's more, you can dramatically shorten the number of years you'll be paying that mortgage. Here's some simple math: If you have a $200,000, 30-year mortgage at 6% and you pay an extra $100 a month, you'll pay off that mortgage in less than 25 years. You'll also save nearly $50,000 in total interest payments.[48] How much better could your retirement be if you had an extra $50,000 and 5 years to put toward it?

### Consider Renting as an Option

*Renting in retirement.* Nowadays, renting has picked up a caché it hasn't had in anyone's memory. And why not? A 2008 study by the Center for Economic Policy Research concluded that those who were renting homes in 2004 will have more wealth in 2009 than people who owned homes in 2004.[49] That's true across all income groups that were profiled, from the poorest to the wealthiest, and it may provide a lesson for anyone preparing to retire...and even for those who are retired. Many retirees "downsize" upon retirement, moving from a big home with lots of room for children to a smaller house that's perfect for a retired couple. For retirees who don't have a lot of equity in their homes, renting a smaller house could be a smart financial move, and one many might not have considered prior to the meltdown. Aside from not shouldering the costs associated with homeownership, a retiree who downsizes and rents may pay much less than they would on a mortgage and have more income for retirement.

In 2009, Nancy Hartman, age 65, retired from her hospital administrator job, and pocketed the gains from the sale of her three-bedroom Dayton, Ohio home. She's now renting a smaller but luxurious condo in Columbus near her grandchildren. *"I'm getting a lot more for my money...and a lot more out of retirement,"* Hartman said.

*Relocation, relocation, relocation.* With unemployment skyrocketing over the last ten years, millions of workers are being forced to relocate to find new jobs. In a booming economy, relocation is often an opportunity to trade up and even benefit from a company "relo" package. Unfortunately, attractive relocation packages are not plentiful in our current recession. With high-paying positions at a premium right now, companies may be reluctant to help you sell your home and cover closing costs—a fairly standard practice in better times. Even if you are fortunate enough to sell your home, you may take a loss to move your family across the country. With your housing situation in transition, consider "relo" renting. There are a number of financial factors to consider in the buying versus renting scenario, and the housing market you move to will be the primary driver. Check out the calculator at *move.com* for more details on how to calculate a price-to-rent ratio.

Whether retiring or relocating, don't worry about availability. For those choosing to rent, the vacancy rate for apartments is 7.5%, the highest level since 1987.[50] And you don't have to settle for an apartment, either, as owners who can't sell homes and condos are renting. You'll pay less for the same space, too. U.S. rents dipped in the last year, and rent will continue to drop.[51]

### *Don't Rely on House Appreciation for Retirement*

Your house is shelter. It's wood and concrete and drywall. We become emotionally attached to houses because they're usually our biggest investments and because of the memories we have there. Dorothy longed for Auntie Em's house because it was there that she'd find Auntie Em cooking something delicious in the kitchen or pleasantly conversing with Uncle Henry. It wasn't the structure that Dorothy was attached to; it was the people and activity in it. The mentality that someone has to take into homeownership is that the structure will provide shelter, not fund a long retirement.

**YOUR HOME IS NOT A RETIREMENT ACCOUNT.**

## Endnotes

1  Las Vegas Home Store, "Less space: The next frontier in real estate," 2007.

2  ABC News, "The Mortgage Mess: Unscrupulous Lenders, Unsuspecting Borrowers," September 10, 2007.

3  *The Wall Street Journal*, "Your Home Isn't the Nest Egg That You May Think It Is," March 13, 2007.

4  Danter Company, Home Ownership Rates, 1997–2005.

5  *The Economist*, "In come the waves," June 16, 2005.

6  *The Albuquerque Tribune*, "Low income growth, rising prices helped burst housing bubble," September 12, 2007.

7  *Forbes*, "What If Housing Crashed?" September 3, 2001.

8 Ludwig von Mises Institute – *Tu Ne Cede Malis*, "The CRA Scam and its Defenders," April 30, 2008.

9 *The New York Times*, "Fannie Mae Eases Credit To Aid Mortgage Lending," September 30, 1999.

10 *The Orange County Register*, "High roller of home loans," May 20, 2007.

11 *The Wall Street Journal*, "Acorn and the Housing Bubble," November 12, 2009.

12 *The New York Times*, "Lehman Files for Bankruptcy; Merrill Is Sold," September 15, 2008.

13 Yahoo! Finance, The Home Depot Inc. (HD): Historical Prices, Jan. 1, 1997–Jan. 31, 1997 and Dec. 1, 1999–Dec. 31, 1999.

14 *The Wall Street Journal*, "Behind Nardelli's Abrupt Exit," January 4, 2007.

15 *Home Improvement and Garden*, "A Brief History of HGTV," September 17, 2008.

16 Bloomberg, "Moody's, S&P Employees Doubted Ratings, E-mails Say (Update2)," October 22, 2008.

17 *Money Week*, "Three reasons why US house prices have further to fall," September 12, 2007.

18 *New York Post*, "The Dow Has Lost Just About 50% From Highs," February 24, 2009.

19 Shiller, Robert, <u>The Subprime Solution</u>, Princeton University Press, August 4, 2008.

20 CNN Money, "Foreclosures: 'Worst three months of all time,'" October 15, 2009.

21 CNN Money, "Home prices slide 14%," Study in article by the National Association of Realtors (NAR), May 12, 2009.

22 *Phoenix Business Journal*, "Slide in Phoenix home values slows," June 30, 2009.

23 Mortgage Bankers Association, "Delinquencies Continue to Climb, Foreclosures Flat in Latest MBA National Delinquency Survey," August 20, 2009.

24 Center for Responsible Lending, "Soaring Spillover: Accelerating Foreclosures To Cost Neighbors $502 Billion in 2009 Alone; 69.5 Million Homes Lose $7,200 On Average," May 7, 2009.

25 *The Orange County Register*, "High roller of home loans," May 20, 2007.

26 Yahoo! Finance, The Home Depot Inc. (HD): Historical Prices, Jan. 1, 1999–Dec. 31, 1999.

27 Yahoo! Finance, The Home Depot, Inc. (HD): Historical Prices, Jan. 1, 2008–Dec. 31, 2008.

28 Yahoo! Finance, Lowe's Companies Inc. (LOW): Historical Prices, Jan. 1, 2006–Dec. 31, 2009.

29  *Time*, "The Networks Look Ahead: Change, the Channel," June 1, 2009.

30  National Foundation for Credit Counseling, "Survey Reveals Long-Term Implications of Mortgage Meltdown," June 23, 2009.

31  *The Wall Street Journal*, "Home-Equity Borrowing Stalls As the Housing Market Cools," April 30, 2007.

32  *Forbes*, "What If Housing Crashed?" September 3, 2001.

33  *Mortgage Magazine*, "As Home Values Rise, Spending on Home Improvement Projects Continues to Grow," October 27, 2005.

34  U.S. Law.com, Definition of Redlining, 2009.

35  McKinley, Vern, "Community Reinvestment Act: Ensuring Credit Adequacy or Enforcing Credit Allocation?" Regulation, 1994 Number 4.

36  McKinley, Vern, "Community Reinvestment Act: Ensuring Credit Adequacy or Enforcing Credit Allocation?" Regulation, 1994 Number 4.

37  Portfolio.com, "The End," November 11, 2008.

38  Portfolio.com, "The End," November 11, 2008.

39  *USA Today*, "Some homeowners struggle to keep up with adjustable rates," April 3, 2006.

40  *The Washington Post*, "'No Money Down' Falls Flat," March 14, 2007.

41  McClatchy Washington Bureau, "Worse than subprime? Other mortgages imploding slowly," June 18, 2009.

42  Realty Times, "Interest Only Loans Part I: The First-Time Home Buyer," October 14, 2004.

43  McClatchy Washington Bureau, "Worse than subprime? Other mortgages imploding slowly," June 18, 2009.

44  Bankrate.com, "Interest-only mortgage deja vu," May 12, 2005.

45  Zweig, Jason, Your Money & Your Brain, Simon & Schuster, 2007.

46  Bankrate.com, "What is a credit score?" March 31, 2005.

47  Hipotecas Prestamos Mortgages, "Obama Foreclosure Programs," November 11, 2009.

48  Wise Bread, "DIY Mortgage Acceleration," May 30, 2007.

49  Center for Economic and Policy Research, "The Housing Crash and the Retirement Prospects of Late Baby Boomers," June 2008.

50  *Reuters*, "U.S. apartment vacancies near historic high: report," July 8, 2009.

51  Yahoo! Finance, "Rents Drop Nationwide as Vacancies Spike," January 23, 2009.

# 5

# Family Matters

---

**KINPHOBIA:** [kin-*foh*-bee-uh]
Fear of having to dig into retirement money to financially help one's family, for example, adult children, siblings, in-laws, or aging parents. *When Barry's wife explained to him that her unemployed mother was cashing in her IRA to buy a time share, his kinphobia kicked in.*

---

A well-to-do acquaintance of mine, I'll call him Randall, lived in the pricey neighborhood of Rancho Santa Fe near San Diego. Some surveys list this ZIP code as the most affluent in the country. He told me the following story about coming home one day with his 12-year-old son in the back seat of his Mercedes. He said that for some reason, on this particular day, as they were passing through the entry of their guard-gated village, fiscal reality seemed to dawn on the boy. Expensive Italian and German steel rolled toward them out the exit gates as they entered, and the young man looked out of the tinted windows at the idyllic scene that seemed to be a combination of a *Lawn and Garden* cover page and a promo for *Lifestyles of the Rich and Famous*. As if for the first time, he noticed the crews of landscapers descending upon the sprawling multimillion dollar estates, the large swimming pools, the manicured palm trees, and the numerous individual tennis courts. Taking all of this in, the young man thoughtfully asked his father the following question:

"Dad, are we rich?"

Randall, carefully considering the question, paused, and then answered:

"No, son. I'm rich. And you get to live with me until you're 18."


## At the Heart of Your Finances

You've heard the saying *"family matters."* Does the phrase imply that family means something, representing a dear and important connection binding the members together in a bond of natural entitlement? Or does it refer to family events that are deeply private, personal issues that affect each member? When it comes to finances, the answer is simple—it's both. Family matters take on even greater importance when we consider our nation's recent economic downturn. For years, the phrase *"play now, pay later"* has been casually tossed around when referring to the Baby Boomer Generation. And in many ways, such an attitude is easily understandable. Having watched their parents set aside money for a lifetime at the expense of enjoying their money, Boomers embraced an entirely different attitude: They spent. And the Pepsi Generation, *"who had a lot to live,"* spent en masse and on the entire family.

In a recent *Money* survey, 54% of Boomer parents admitted their kids have too much stuff, and they spend too much on their children.[1] One of our focus group couples commented:

> *"We both spend too much on our kids. Video games, cameras, bikes, and riding lessons—you name it. We want them to have what we didn't have growing up. I suppose we spoil them. Birthdays and holidays are very special at our house."*

Another one of our Boomer focus group participants spoke about spending close to $1,500 on a laptop for his son who is in seventh grade, and it made him wonder. *"Would I spend that much on myself?"* he asked. No. Would his parents have spent that much on him? The answer is no again. It's not that his parents didn't want him to have the best, but like most parents of Boomers, the *"Greatest*

*Generation,"* as Tom Brokaw coined them, they were savers rather than spenders. As survivors of the Great Depression, they were extremely frugal, worked hard and had very little disposable income. They didn't have enough resources to buy things that weren't necessities, and in many cases spent most of their lives living paycheck to paycheck. This modest lifestyle translated directly into fairly conservative and shorter retirement lives. Unlike Boomers, however, the previous generation had pension plans that were still active, could count on Social Security and probably didn't enter a long retirement with high spending expectations and a mountain of debt.

Many Boomers can give examples of spoiling their kids in various ways, but here are some stories from my personal experience...and yes, some of these stories fall into the *"walk to school through the snow"* type category:

1. *Bicycles.* When I was a kid, the four of us shared a single large, blue, balloon-tired, girl's bicycle that my parents had purchased used. It weighed about 300 pounds, and for years, it was the only bicycle in the house. For the younger kids, it was impossible to sit on the seat. You rode standing up or not at all. All four kids learned to ride on that bike. I have lost count of the number of bicycles I have purchased for my kids—as I have tried to perfectly match their newly achieved growth to the correctly sized bicycle.

2. *Restaurants.* Unless we were on vacation, it was a rare occasion when we went out to a meal as a kid. If my dad was feeling particularly extravagant, he took us to a place called The Flaming Pit in Village Square—a strip mall in a St. Louis suburb. It would be the equivalent of perhaps a Black Angus today. We dressed for the occasion, too—about the same as if going to church. Tell my kids today that we're going out to eat, and you will hear a chorus of groans. "Why can't we just stay here? We want to see this new DVD, and I just got this new game."

3. *Creatures.* I had three stuffed toys when I was a kid—a Huckleberry Hound, a boxer dog (okay, I called it Boxer Doggie), and a teddy bear. I stacked all three at the foot of my bed each night—until my dog ate some of them. I am embarrassed to say that I can't even tell you how many of these things my children have—but I think the number is approximately equal to the size of the Chinese army—dolls, Pokémon things,

Build-A-Bears, Webkins, action figures, and things I can't even name.

4. *Space.* Until she left the house as a young teen, my wife shared a single small bedroom with her two sisters. Right now, my three kids each have their own room and are convinced that they are "crammed" into that space.

Many of you could probably add dozens of similar examples.

*"My parents were both frugal as well because they grew up in the Depression, and they talked about walking along the road picking up pop cans, back then it was bottles, to make ends meet. They saved quite a bit. I probably spend more than they do. They had their house paid for at the age that I am, and I don't. But I probably have an equivalent amount saved up as what they did. My dad was a workaholic, so retirement for him was kind of a difficult thing to do. When he finally did, [my parents] did well."*

—Male Focus Group Participant

With more disposable income and a taste for spending, Boomers differ significantly from their parents with respect *to* and respect *for* money. There's an expression that goes *"More money, more problems,"* and family typically complicates that dynamic. Because money can be such a difficult and touchy subject, many married Boomer couples avoid talking about it, especially if a couple is deep in debt. Unfortunately, the longer a couple avoids this topic, the greater the problem becomes. At our focus groups, some couples would say they agreed on spending limits. Sounds good. Then we asked them to individually write down their spending limit on a piece of paper and share it with their spouse. As a result of that exercise, we had some surprised husbands and wives. One husband admitted he bought a $500 set of golf clubs without consulting his wife, and then, as if in retaliation, his upset wife pronounced that she bought $250 worth of clothes online.

*"What can I say...I like new clothes. My husband hits the roof when I run up our credit cards, but we've never discussed a limit. But he just spent $500 on golf clubs and didn't tell me. He hid them in the trunk of his car."*

Another couple, both surprised by the number their spouse wrote down, seemed okay with the higher than expected numbers because they both worked and earned money.

*"I don't know what our limit is...we both work, so we both pay bills and we both spend money, so we haven't established any rules, even though we've been married for ten years."*

But it brings up a very interesting question. What if there is a difference of opinion between spouses on spending limits, and more importantly, what if that limit is quite large—maybe even thousands or tens of thousands of dollars apart? Perhaps the ultimate form of "psychological layering" is giving *carte blanche* to another individual—like a spouse. Especially when the other spouse does not review related financial statements.

A financial setup that allows for another individual to spend freely and in any magnitude, without having complete awareness of the money being spent, seems like the ultimate insulation. Think about a spouse, for example, who gives the other spouse the green light for a landscaping facelift and then arrives home a few weeks later to find a 12-man work crew with jackhammers, cement mixers, and dozens of plants, trees, and fresh rolls of sod. Without having discussed a budget or placed parameters on the scope of the project, the spouse who okayed the project has no right to be upset.

The point is, without communication, accountability, and perhaps financial guidance, the whole family loses, especially when planning for retirement. According to new research, 85% of couples lack confidence in each other's ability to manage finances. And on critical retirement decisions, couples are simply not on the same page: 60% don't agree on their respective retirement ages; nearly 50% can't agree if they will work in retirement; and 42% have different ideas regarding their expected lifestyle in retirement.[2]

But these failures to communicate are just the beginning of their problems. Their parents used to hold onto their money because they'd felt the sting of the Great Depression; they knew what hard times really were. They lived well within their means and made sure they always had access to money in case of emergency. They were there to help their Boomer children with college tuition, a down payment for a house, or the seed money for a college fund. The Boomers, conversely, looked upon their parents as a constant financial resource, to be tapped whenever there was a need or even a want.

When it came to money, members of the Greatest Generation were proud and self-sufficient. They didn't all give money to their Boomer children or provide a financial backstop, but they did impart good financial sense that wasn't always heeded. And when that financial sense wasn't heeded by their Boomer kids, it became especially difficult for those in the unenviable position of caring for aging parents and paying for kids in college simultaneously.

# The Club Sandwich Generation

The financial burdens on families are not solely relegated to financial and inheritance decisions. Just ask anyone raising kids and caring for aging parents at the same time.

As the Sandwich Generation, Boomers have been stuck in the middle for years. Now, spikes in longevity, coupled with the effect of the recent meltdown, have given rise to what could be called the *Club Sandwich Generation*. We are seeing more layers to this family sandwich than ever before with four- and five-generation families becoming more common. Nearly 10 million Boomers are now actively engaged in raising children while providing financial support for one or more aging parents.[3] Many feel trapped in the middle, and rightly so. On a daily basis, they can be found balancing the tasks of getting the kids off to school while managing mom's prescription regimen and doctor appointments. And by all indications, becoming a caregiver for a parent today may require as many or more years than actually spent raising a child.

The toll on families can be staggering, and adults caring for aging parents often struggle with a wide range of mixed emotions. It's difficult to watch a person you love who was once capable and competent lose his independence. For those witnessing such a decline, sadness often follows, with 91% reporting depression.[4] In addition to the emotional burden, becoming the parent of a parent can also bring a heavy physical toll. Caregivers report chronic conditions such as high blood pressure at nearly twice the rate of other Americans.[5] The pressures of today's fragmented families also weigh heavily in the mix, with single moms and dads increasingly caring for an aging parent while trying to hold down a day job. For most, that leaves little time for themselves or any chance of having a social life of their own. On top of it all, when regular income isn't enough, many are forced to tap into their retirement accounts just to pay the bills.

> *"My greatest fear,"* said one 64-year-old female from our focus groups, *"is having to move into the room over my son's garage. Unfortunately, that's my son's greatest fear as well."*

Even when aging parents have the funds to cover their expenses, many fall prey to mistakes and outright fraud. According to the U.S. Office of Community Oriented Policing Services in 2008, consumer fraud estimates show that between 20% and 60% of adults report being a victim or attempted victim of fraud.[6] Older Americans tend to be better targets for scams because they have accumulated a lifetime of assets, and more often than not, they have the spare time to attend seminars and listen to pitches. The problem then cascades down to their adult children who not only must spend time trying to recover lost funds, but also suddenly find themselves supporting their parents who no longer have the money to care for their own financial needs.

# How a Sandwich Becomes a Club Sandwich

Liz Monroe, a woman participating in our focus group research, knows from experience how the best-laid plans can be forced to evolve when a Baby Boomer suddenly finds herself in the middle of the Club Sandwich Generation. After living in Colorado for more than 30 years, Liz moved back home to New England to be near her family. She felt fortunate because both of her parents were still alive and healthy, her siblings were married with children, and there appeared to be many years of joy for her to spend more closely with the family.

> *"I guess you could say that I have been a primary caregiver for the family since I was a teenager," said Liz. "Like most Baby Boomers, I come from a relatively large family. I was the oldest of five children. My parents owned a real estate office, and both my mom and dad worked many, many hours. As a result, growing up I was often leaned on to babysit my younger brothers and sister."* When Liz turned 18, she became the first member of her family to attend college when she moved across the country to enroll at Colorado College. It was in Colorado that she met her husband, started a family, and laid roots for the next 30 years.

By the time her own son had graduated from college, Liz was ready to move home to live close to her parents, her siblings, nephews, nieces, and cousins. *"My parents were in their seventies and retired. I knew they wouldn't live forever, but I was excited to be near them as they enjoyed their golden years, and as I started the countdown to my own retirement,"* Liz said. The series of unfortunate events that would soon follow had significant ramifications for Liz, both emotionally and financially. Within a couple years, one of her brothers unexpectedly passed away, leaving her parents as the guardians for a preteen granddaughter. Shortly thereafter, Liz's father passed away, too. Liz immediately moved into a larger house with a mother-in-law apartment and asked her 77-year-old mother and middle-school aged niece to come live with her.

It was a big surprise when Liz's mother again found love and, at the ripe age of 80, remarried. Her stepfather moved in with the family. Shortly thereafter, another of Liz's brothers fell onto hard times, and he and his newborn baby moved in with Liz, too. With the countdown to Liz's retirement rapidly approaching, she suddenly found herself as the head of household for a growing family, albeit in an untraditional manner. Liz, her teenage niece, mother, stepfather, younger brother, and infant nephew were all living under one roof. The Club Sandwich was officially complete, and Liz was now responsible for a multigenerational household ranging from 3 months to 80 years.

Within a few years, Liz's mother passed away. Unfortunately, Liz never knew much about her mother's finances in spite of the years they spent living together. *"For our generation, it was never considered appropriate for the children, even as adults, to talk with our parents about things like sources of income, debts, assets, or wills. It just wasn't something we discussed."* Nevertheless, Liz was named executor of her mother's estate. There was no will and testament. With no financial or legal experience to speak of, Liz found herself thrust into having the responsibility for

- Planning and paying for her mother's funeral
- Tracking down and securing assets from five different banks and insurance companies
- Sorting out inaccurate beneficiary designations on many accounts that still reflected her previously deceased father as beneficiary
- Equitably distributing assets across the remaining four siblings and the two children of her deceased brother
- Equitably distributing family heirlooms to siblings, her stepfather, and a long line of other grandchildren, cousins, nieces, nephews, godchildren, and so on.

After a crash course in financial basics, and with the help of an experienced and credentialed estate planner, Liz was finally able to sort through her mother's finances. It took nearly a year to uncover everything and to get some brokerage houses and insurance companies to pay out her mother's assets. Some of them required copies of long-lost death certificates, powers-of-attorney, and other important documents—in many cases Liz did not know if they existed or where they were kept. Several companies wanted to meet with Liz and try to sell her new products at a time when she was feeling most confused and vulnerable.

*"Neither I, nor my siblings, really had a good feel for what to do, or what our mother would have wanted," said Liz. "Fortunately, we are an extremely close-knit family with very strong and secure relationships. Together, we navigated the difficult and confusing times. I can only imagine how much more traumatic this whole experience would have been if we did not have open lines of communication and trust in one another."*

Despite eventually sorting through her mother's final affairs, Liz still has a long road ahead. She has spent her peak earning years trying to balance her own retirement plan with expenses for her mother's medical and long-term care needs, providing support and care for her infant nephew, and planning to pay for her niece's college tuition. Compounding matters, as she counted down what she thought were the final two years before retirement, her employer—the state of Rhode Island—recently announced a massive overhaul to the state pension program, which will significantly change the amount of retirement income Liz can expect, as well as when she can start receiving it.

*"Looking back on my experiences, I definitely had some unexpected curveballs thrown my way," Liz concluded. "But when it comes to being there and helping take care of my family, there is nothing I would have done differently. Except I do think we could have saved ourselves some big headaches if we had just done more to make sure my parents and siblings were all on the same page when it came to estate planning and the family's finances...and I wish I had forced myself to set aside a little more money for my own retirement."*

Dependence on family for financial support in difficult times is nothing new, though it's rarely discussed. That's probably because it's never been a great source of pride for any of the parties involved, no matter what their financial situation is. After all, sometimes that financial support is there just to keep up appearances.

In their book, *The Millionaire Next Door,* authors Stanley and Danko refer to Economic Outpatient Care (EOC) as the economic gifts that some parents give their adult children and grandchildren. As America grays, it will be considerably more difficult for the aging affluent to keep subsidizing their adult children, especially those millions devastated beyond recovery by the meltdown. Although some of these financial gifts are used for extra toppings, such as private schools, country club memberships, and luxury automobiles, many families have come to depend on EOC just to maintain their current lifestyle, such as making mortgage payments and paying for daycare. As eldercare replaces elder income, family bonds and future generations will be tested like never before. In his much-heralded 1991 novel, *Generation X*, Douglas Coupland dubbed the phrase *"pull-the-plug, slice the pie."*[7] He defines this as a popular mental game for 20-somethings that involves fantasizing about how much their parents are worth. Indeed, the exercise may be picking up some new practitioners—whether or not they will admit to it. Reverse mortgage loan officers can tell you that one of the most common obstacles to the elderly obtaining these loans is that quite often, younger family members do everything in their power to convince grandma not to do it. The sphere of family influence can provide a baseline that encompasses a broad spectrum of financial challenges—challenges that are more exposed, more complicated, and more likely to affect retirement than ever before.

Before the meltdown, expectations were high for multiple generations to depend on family for financial support.

- Faith in the markets would translate into a comfortable retirement and adequate money for college.
- Generation X and Boomers were counting on an inheritance.
- Families focused on leaving a legacy.
- Ninety-two percent of affluent Boomer parents financially helped their adult children.[8]

    70% helped with college loans

    52% helped with a car purchase

    41% paid for car insurance

    35% made car payments

After the meltdown, millions of families are facing new realities as they live with new economic uncertainties.

- Families are struggling with new financial realities, including heavy losses in many retirement accounts and more prosaic expectations for future investment returns.
- Fifty-eight percent of the preretirement group, the highest of any age group, said the recession had caused them family stress. Three-quarters of those over 65 said they still plan to leave money or property to their kids or family, albeit a reduced amount.[9]
- Derailed college plans threaten adequate funds for school.
- More than 40% of American families are now burdened with eldercare. It is estimated that 34 million Americans today serve as unpaid caregivers for other adults, usually elderly relatives, and that they spend an average of 21 hours a week helping out. The economic impact of this "free" care was about $350 billion in 2006. That's more than the U.S. government spent on Medicare in 2005 and exceeded the size of the federal budget deficit in 2006. The National Alliance for Caregiving estimates that $659,000 per person is lost in pensions, Social Security benefits, and wages as adult children take time off of work to care for their parents.[10]
- Thirty-three percent of those aged 18–49 live with their parents or in-laws.[11]

We should all try to recognize that a number of significant financial mistakes can be traced back to family in one form or another. No surprise, right? What might come as a surprise is just how deeply those influences can affect your chances of achieving a successful retirement. And that sphere of family influence can provide a baseline that encompasses a broad spectrum of not only challenges, but also opportunities. From our parents' treatment of money to the sudden windfall an inheritance might bring, understanding the implications of family money can be a crucial component for today's retirees and preretirees.

Family communication, education, and understanding are just a few of the components that can add to the success or failure of managing family money. Although all families are unique, two behavioral finance concepts that can be attributed to motivation and behavioral mistakes within families are *familiarity bias* and *attachment bias*.

# The Retirement Brain Game

**Familiarity bias**—In a series of experiments conducted in 1991, behavioral finance experts Amos Tversky and Chip Heath showed that when people have a choice between two gambles, they will pick the more familiar gamble, even if the odds are against them.[12] *And what's more familiar than family?* Families can be extremely influential in the way we view money.

**Attachment bias**—When we become emotionally attached to a security or an investment style, we may be succumbing to what is referred to as *attachment bias*. This bias can be seen when adult children invest the way the family has always invested. Coca-Cola stock worked well for dad, so why shouldn't it work well for me? The way that their parents invested may have been appropriate for them but, in most cases, will not be suitable for their adult children. The simple fact is that an income-producing strategy for a retiree generally should not be the same strategy for those approaching or planning for retirement. For subsequent generations inheriting family money, the *attachment bias* serves to constrict the fluid movement of capital toward constructive and appropriate investment portfolios.

### All Too Familiar

When it comes to family matters, **familiarity bias** can get very personal and very disruptive to investment and business decisions. Here's what one of our focus group participants had to say about her husband's family business.

> "My husband maintained his family business with his father and brother. It was a camera shop and they really knew cameras. And they provided the kind of personal and professional service that customers can't get at the discount stores. Problem was that technology changed, and people could buy

*easy-to-use digital cameras cheaper and didn't need the per-sonal touch. They loved working together, but the business never changed and it failed. It was a shame, but we lost a lot of money."*

—Female Focus Group Participant

*Familiarity bias* extends beyond the family as well but rarely strays too far from home. In 2007, Shlomo Benartzi found that *nearly 80% of employees believed the company they worked for was less risky than average.*[13] From this research, we can conclude that work-ers are comfortable with the company they work for, and perhaps more importantly, with what they are familiar with. Familiarity could be considered a key component to contentment and productivity. Take the military, for example. In a WWII German U-Boat, the crews were often out at sea for months at a time in shockingly tight quarters. Despite the premium on space and weight, the U-boats were engi-neered with several wooden arches across the ceiling—even though they served absolutely no functional purpose. At that time, typical crew members were unfamiliar with steel structures. They were accustomed to the structural strength of dwellings being provided through wood and stone. Hence, the arches were put there exclu-sively for the crew's psychological comfort—just like there is comfort in making a financial and emotional investment in what we are famil-iar with, whether it is the company we work for, or the company we keep, especially family.

The *familiarity bias* can cause problems for investors who hold onto businesses or stocks that are no longer performing well. When you keep the familiar, because you've always been comfortable with it, like a family stock for example, you may have a tendency to under-estimate how risky the stock is and fail to diversify your portfolio. One behavioral finance study shows that people rank their home country's economy higher than the economies of other countries.[14] In college football, coaches and the media are asked to rank teams in weekly polls, which is very subjective, and often the teams that are ranked are the ones the coaches and media see most often on TV, or are the teams they are most familiar with. Finally, in the preceding camera shop example, the father and sons knew cameras, but their comfort with what was familiar blinded the big picture, and ultimately those blinders contributed to the failure of their family business.

### The Family Ties That Bind

**Attachment bias** can cause a lot of family financial issues as well. This behavior is what keeps us anchored to the traditional stocks and bonds of our parents' generation. Take inheritance, for instance. Many investors tend to hold onto inherited money "as is," and thereby allow inertia to be the driving strategy behind inherited investment money. Think of it this way: My favorite breed of dog has always been the Airedale Terrier. Airedales are intelligent, brave, tenacious, and have a great sense of humor. In spite of their hunting skill, however, a purebred Airedale is no good at retrieving. I've had plenty of baseballs, tennis balls, slippers, and other things that have wound up in the jaws of an Airedale, never to return because the Airedale, by instinct, becomes so attached to his new possession. Investors can be like Airedales in their emotional attachments to a security, business, or property, especially when family ties are involved.

A focus group survey underlines the consequences of this bias. Married couples were asked if they had treated inherited money differently than other sources of income. One of the surveyed wives had inherited money from her grandparents and insisted on keeping the money in a savings account at a credit union. She contended that the money would be safe there and could be used later to help pay for their son's college. Her husband objected, feeling the money could earn a much higher rate of return if invested. However, his wife remained sentimentally attached to the money her grandparents had worked so hard to earn and wanted it in a very safe place even though a savings account did not match their overall investment strategy.

*"I said let's do stocks, bonds, anything but a bank account, but she (my wife) wouldn't budge on it. What a waste. I think [the bank] was paying maybe 1.2% or 1.5%, something that effective. It was senseless."*

—Husband, Married Couple Interview

There's no question that psychological biases can negatively impact an inheritance, but mishandling "found money" can be just as, if not more, dangerous. As I covered, people can be overly sentimental with family inheritance, leading to mistakes like holding onto a losing stock, keeping a company that isn't profitable, and being overly conservative with investments.

Conversely, an inheritance can be treated like house money, the effect we covered in Chapter 3, "The NoZone." In this case, the windfall is more like a winning lottery ticket than a sacred family honor. Consider the comments of another focus group participant whose cousin inherited money.

> *"I have a cousin whose father died, and she inherited between $10,000 and $15,000. By God, she threw it away like it was running water. Bought herself a used car for "X" amount of thousands, bought her ex-husband a used car for "X" amount, and before you know it, she went through that $10,000 or $15,000 like that, and it was gone in no time. Personally, I would have dug into some sort of real estate investments, some stocks, even if it were as safe as Pepsi or Coke, and done something constructive with it."*

—Male Focus Group Participant

Sadly, this same scenario plays out over and over throughout the country on a daily basis. If the person in the preceding example had made a more prudent decision, such as investing the inheritance in the market, she could have made strides toward retirement. The financial mistakes that can accompany intergenerational wealth transfer become an even greater problem when the sums are larger and are often exacerbated by the differing mentalities that already divide the generations.

### Earned Money Versus Found Money

For those who earned, planned, invested, and saved over a lifetime, their nest eggs have a deeper value. Their portfolios are viewed as concrete, tangible assets. Savers understand the time and effort it takes to amass the money. And as a result, such transparency lends itself to careful, conscious decision making.

However, the opposite can be true when we examine inheritance and windfall recipients. For them, there is often considerably less appreciation for the work it took to earn or amass the funds. The overall value of inherited money becomes less tangible; we may be too sentimental with it, or we may have diminished respect for funds that we didn't earn over time. Either way, judgment can be clouded and mistakes made.

| Transparent | Opaque | Takeaway |
|---|---|---|
| Earned Money | Found Money | |
| Money that is earned is likely used for budgeted expenses such as mortgage, car payments, and utilities. | Money that is inherited may be used too conservatively if there is an attachment bias, or too aggressively if it is treated like house money. | To maximize your financial potential, money should be treated the same, whether it is earned, inherited, or won. |

# Improve Your Retirementology IQ

We've looked at a number of family money challenges and how our innate psychological biases can impact the decision-making process. Let's take a look at some of the steps you can take to deal more effectively with family matters.

## Inheritance: Avoid the "Three-and-Out" Dilemma

There are many complexities involved in how money is transferred between generations. In many cases, inheritance encompasses the tiny details that can make the difference between keeping your money in the family and losing it to spending blunders, investment errors, and costly tax consequences. Some studies indicate that a family's wealth is usually dissipated within about three generations—the thinking being that the first generation earns the money while the second generation gets to enjoy it. Because the second generation didn't earn the money, they may have less respect for how to handle it. By the third generation, family members have no concept of the discipline needed to earn the money and may have no financial management skills at all.

When we think about a pending inheritance, or passing family money to the next generation, avoiding the "three-and-out" dilemma becomes even clearer. There's an overriding concern among many families about how *not to lose* an inheritance. Parents may worry about how to divide the funds among children. Many also worry about leaving large sums to younger children, or the possibility that poor spending habits or costly life events, such as divorce, may dangerously erode the funds. These concerns are as valid as the steps to addressing them.

The first step is to encourage an open family environment where money can be discussed. For many families, this can be intimidating. Families must resolve to openly discuss their hopes for what can be accomplished with family money. Discussions need to be interactive with an emphasis on defining the family's values and mission for the money. The big myth to recognize and avoid is that by talking about money with kids, they will gain a sense of entitlement. The reality is quite the opposite. And never be fooled into thinking family money conversations are one-time events. They should be an ongoing process. The last thing anyone wants is for their kids to one day be stuck in a financial squeeze that could have been avoided with proper discussion, planning, and resources.

We shouldn't overlook another basic step with children, the lack of general fiscal responsibility and understanding. Let's face it; we can't count on schools to teach children the importance of budgeting or balancing their checkbook. Whether it is through handling an inheritance or managing their day-to-day spending options, we need to take responsibility in the home for educating our kids. That way, they will be prepared to make prudent financial decisions as adults.

A final step toward the successful inheritance and transfer of family money is to talk frequently and candidly about how the family got its money or how the family business operates. The key in such discussions is to encourage a consensus around how the family can best take care of future generations. Rather than falling prey to the "three-and-out" tendency for family money, we should create multigenerational thinking. We must let future generations know that we were thinking about them, and they in turn should think about the generation behind them. In this way, family money can become a lasting legacy.

Windfall and inheritance recipients often find themselves on an emotional roller coaster after coming into a large sum of unexpected money. One might expect typical emotional responses to include excitement, exuberance, and elation. But some of the more common emotions actually include guilt, shame, isolation, and fear.

### Take a Decision-Making Timeout

Think of it as a financial sabbatical. The money is new to you, and you're new to it. And it's not going anywhere soon. So, create a safe place to work through your emotions as well as your options.

### Take Stock of Your Identity

Don't redefine or reinvent yourself. If your inheritance is large, keep a level head. The only thing sudden wealth should change is your ability to achieve your retirement goals that much sooner.

### Protect Your Legacy—B.O.S.S.

One of the most common financial planning errors impacting families today is also one of the errors most frequently overlooked. It is the issue of incorrect beneficiary designations on financial products, including mutual funds, retirement accounts, IRAs, life insurance, and annuities. Such beneficiary designation errors can have severe, unanticipated consequences, including needless expenses and taxes; potential of disinheriting children or grandchildren; and delays in providing for the financial needs of loved ones. Unfortunately, most people do not realize they have a problem until it is too late.

Fortunately, although a potentially devastating risk to your family's finances, the issue can be one of the most straightforward and easy to rectify.

The use of a simple acronym (B.O.S.S.) can be helpful in illustrating the issue. No, B.O.S.S. is not just the person you work for, although it certainly can have a more lasting impact on you and your family than any employer ever would. B.O.S.S. is an acronym standing for

**B**eneficiary

**O**wner

**S**pouse

**S**urvivor

These four key designations need to be completed accurately on most financial accounts to make sure your assets pass to desired heirs at the right time and in an efficient manner. Estate-planning experts indicate that there are four common errors with B.O.S.S.: 1) Failing to update beneficiary designations; 2) Failing to name a contingent beneficiary; 3) Naming the estate as the beneficiary, and 4) Owning assets jointly.

### Failing to Update Beneficiary Designations

One of the most common—and easily avoidable—errors is simply failing to update beneficiary designations. If you have experienced any of the following, it is time to work with an adviser to review and update all your financial account forms:

- Change in marital status
- Birth of a child or grandchild
- Death in the family
- Health problem
- Relocation
- New job or promotion

## Failing to Name a Contingent Beneficiary

Another common mistake is failing to name, or maintain, accurate contingent beneficiary designations. If the primary beneficiary predeceases the account owner or insured, the proceeds are paid to the estate, which may subject the assets to probate with double taxation and creditor access ensuing. Also, there may be estate-planning scenarios where it's advantageous for the primary beneficiary to disclaim their right to the inherited asset. Contingent beneficiary designations play an important role in these situations. A general recommendation may be to employ the "Rule of Two." Name two backups for every person named on the account as a beneficiary. This way all parties involved know who the assets will pass to, and you can usually avoid having the assets become subject to probate.

## Naming the Estate as the Beneficiary

By naming the estate as the beneficiary, you guarantee that the precious dollars that you want to go to your loved ones will be subject to the delays, expenses, and public scrutiny associated with probate. In addition, your assets may not go to the right person, in the right amount, or at the right time, resulting in the potential disinheritance of your heirs and certainly the unnecessary delays and expenses associated with probate. Probate is a process whereby your will, assuming you have one, is presented to the court, and an executor or administrator is appointed to pay final expenses and to carry out the terms of the will. If there is no will, state law dictates how the estate will be distributed. Either way, the process can take months or even years to determine where your assets go.

## Owning Assets Jointly

For obvious reasons, the majority of assets owned by married couples are held jointly. This arrangement acts as a "poor man's will," and on the surface, jointly held property may seem like the right idea. But it can become a nightmare, possibly resulting in higher estate taxes and even the possibility of unintentionally disinheriting loved ones. The risk of higher estate taxes arises because jointly held assets pass directly to the surviving spouse, nullifying the deceased's estate tax exclusion ($3.5 million in 2009)[15] and potentially triggering needless taxes when the second spouse passes away. Furthermore, the surviving spouse can bequeath the property at death to anyone she wants, regardless of the desires of the original deceased spouse. This loss of control can be especially horrendous if a spouse remarries or there are children from a previous marriage.

So how can you help avoid these types of errors? First, gather all the pertinent financial documents, including copies of your beneficiary forms, title documents, insurance contracts, annuity contracts, custodial agreements, and retirement plan summary descriptions. Second, review these documents to ensure that they are up to date, in proper order, and will fulfill the objectives of your overall plan. Third, inform your beneficiaries. You may want to schedule a meeting with your adviser to review your financial plans with your beneficiaries so that they will understand the options they have when they inherit your assets. There are a lot of rules, laws, and considerations that should be reviewed to ensure your financial and estate plans fulfill all your objectives and maximize the legacy you pass to your heirs.

Clearly, matters of the family are more complex for Baby Boomers than any previous generation. Significant concerns rightfully exist regarding eldercare for a parent intersecting with preparing for a child's education, on top of financial planning for one's own retirement. The sandwiching and even "club sandwiching" of a generation is in full effect and may be one of the greatest financial risks facing us all. One of the best things you can do today to minimize future headaches for you and your loved ones is to work with an adviser to develop a clear understanding of

- What documents do I need?
- How will my beneficiaries find these documents?
- Are beneficiary and contingent beneficiaries listed and current?
- Who will advise my beneficiaries?

Although a clear plan and good documentation may not solve all your family's private and personal issues, a good roadmap and organized documentation can help ensure everybody is on the same page with respect to financial family matters, which can help the family navigate important financial and tax hurdles along the way.

### Set Family Spending Limits and Guidelines

The most important spending rule for couples is to communicate.

- Meet once or twice a week to discuss budget and financial issues.
- Be honest with each other about spending and set limits.
- Divide responsibilities.

### Forget the Joneses—They're Broke

Prior to the 20th century, social status was measured by the family name. *"Keeping up with the Joneses"* refers to the desire to be seen as being as good as our neighbors by comparing status and is not only bad for your fiscal fitness, it can be hazardous to your physical health. In a study titled *Social Comparisons and Health: Can Having Richer Friends Make You Sick?*, University of Chicago researchers asked 3,005 men and women—ages 57 to 85—to rate their health and list individual illnesses, such as heart problems and diabetes.[16] They were also asked to rate their financial position in their social network of friends, family, neighbors, and workmates. Analysis showed that those very low in the pecking order were up to 22% more likely to be in poor health than those who *believed* they had done the best for themselves.[17] But being at the other end of the social spectrum cut the risk of diabetes, ulcers, and high blood pressure. Another good reason to forget the Joneses...they're probably broke. Forty-three percent of American families spend more than they earn.[18]

## Teach Your Children

A young college co-ed came running in tears to her father. *"Dad, you gave me some terrible financial advice!"*

*"I did? What did I tell you?"* asked the dad.

*"You told me to put my money in that big bank, and now that big bank is in trouble."*

*"What are you talking about? That's one of the most stable banks in the state,"* he said. *"There must be some mistake."*

*"I don't think so,"* she sniffed. *"They just returned one of my checks with a note saying, 'Insufficient Funds.'"*[19]

Although this story is amusing, there is a moral. Teach your children about finances as early as possible. The most consistent theme we have heard through the course of our focus groups is that Boomers regret not starting to plan earlier. Planning early can make all the difference in the world for retirement. Please encourage your children to be informed and plan for their financial future as early as possible. A great way to educate your children on financial literacy is to get them involved in Junior Achievement. Check out its website at www.ja.org.

Also consider these guidelines for educating your children on financial matters:[20]

- Ages 5–9: Teach basic money skills and develop a work ethic.
- Ages 10–13: Teach skills and responsibilities, that is, open up a savings account.
- Ages 14–18: Coach kids on using checking and credit.
- Ages 19–22: Set a path to financial independence.

## Sandwiched? Have a Plan

If you're feeling sandwiched with family matters, it is likely that you are facing special problems you may never have expected. The Sandwich Generation faces what experts have termed the *"financial trifecta"*—preparing for college or paying it off, helping your parents with medical or nursing home expenses, and planning for your own retirement, which may be fast approaching.

Being in the midst of this sandwich can take its emotional toll. Often, siblings disagree on how to help parents or refuse to take part. Children who are approaching adulthood may be placing fresh demands on you. Difficulty finding work and divorce may also send the kids back home. Today, 35% of adults living at home say they had lived independently before having to return home.[21] On top of this, with greater longevity there is often more than one parent who needs care, and frequently on both sides of the family.

By most accounts, many of the Boomers represented in the Sandwich Generation are handling the situation very well. But with just a little help, you can make sure you handle it even better. The first thing you may want to ask yourself is how much of a commitment are you willing and able to make? Take stock of your own abilities and go from there. It may sound odd, but being honest with yourself is every bit as important as being honest with your aging parents.

Next comes the tough part: having an honest chat with all the ingredients of this sandwich. Even if your family has not been strong at communicating previously, now is the time to learn how to change that. When you suspect you may be caring for an aging parent in the near future, be sure to get the facts right away. Avoid surprises later. Ask your parents about their finances, even difficult questions. It is important to be empathetic about your parents' need for privacy, but you also must protect your future. This means ensuring that you have a thorough understanding of your parents' assets. You may want to consider discussing a durable power of attorney for their finances, a healthcare directive, and the possibility of even updating their wills. At the same time, ensure that your adult children have an equal understanding of your complete financial picture and life-planning objectives.

Like discussions about family money with children, a candid financial discussion with a parent should never be a one-time event. Even the most financially literate person can fall prey to the previously discussed scams. To help keep the scam artists at bay, you need to know what your parents are doing with their money. Take an active role with aging parents. Review their bank and credit card statements with them. You'll be glad you did.

As your parents age, it will become very important to make sure you have the legal authority to act swiftly on their behalf in case of an emergency. Consider a durable power of attorney authorizing financial decisions on their behalf and a living will. Explore options for long-term care. Bills for a nursing home or extended home care can easily reach six figures per year. Find out if your parents have long-term care insurance or enough money set aside to cover such costs. But don't forget to take care of yourself. As much as we all want to be there for our parents, it's imperative that we be diligent with our money and don't put our retirement goals on the back burner.

If you are fortunate enough to have these conversations while your parents are still healthy, you will have a greater range of options. For example, you may want to consider making alterations to their living space, whether that is at your home or theirs. Small things like adding handrails in the bathroom or adding ramps where stairs used to be can really make a difference. If they have yet to move into your home, you may want to start planning for the changes you will need to make and start preparing ahead of time.

Another consideration for still-healthy parents might be long-term care insurance. Such a policy promises to pay expenses associated with in-home, assisted living, and nursing home care. Although insurance can provide peace of mind, it's important to be realistic with your own financial situation and make sure you can afford the payments. After all, it's a gamble where you are betting that you might use the policy at some point, and the insurance company is gambling that you won't.

For families facing the prospect of looking for assisted living facilities, you should be aware that the term is applied loosely to a wide range of care options. Thirty years ago, an elderly parent who required full-time care would have only a nursing home as an option. Today, you have many choices, but with them the burden of making a decision will also be yours.

When it comes to paying for the care of an elder or a child, it's equally important to have a handle on where the financing will come from. Consider first exhausting your parents' resources and making sure your parents have long-term care insurance. And seek assistance from social services and from an attorney who specializes in care for the elderly. For the kids, start a college plan or take out loans. Whatever you do, don't stop contributing to your own retirement. Ultimately, the kids will be glad that you thought of yourself first when they become part of the next Club Sandwich Generation.

Finally, when tapping your own or a family member's assets to pay for elder care costs, it's important to think about the order in which you are removing funds. Generally speaking, you'll want to start with withdrawals from taxable accounts first so that tax-deferred accounts can continue to grow. However, there are a host of options and considerations to explore based on your individual situation, and those nuances are best left between you and a qualified adviser familiar with your financial affairs.

**FINANCIAL SUPPORT DECISIONS FOR
EXTENDED FAMILIES MAY HAVE
AN IMPACT ON YOUR RETIREMENT.**

# Endnotes

1  CNN Money, "It's time to unspoil your kids," June 1, 2009.

2  *Boomer Market Advisor*, "Retiring couples can't agree," August 2009.

3  CNN Money, "Sandwich Generation: Survive the midlife tug of war," February 20, 2007.

4  Articlesbase, "I Just Can't Do it Anymore: Depression Associated with Caring for Elderly Parents," January 16, 2009.

5  *USA Today*, "Becoming 'parent of your parent' an emotionally wrenching process," June 24, 2007.

6  U.S. Office of Community Oriented Policing Services, "Financial Crimes Against the Elderly," April 30, 2008.

7  Coupland, Douglas, Generation X, St. Martin's Press, 1991, p. 137.

8  *Aging Well Magazine*, "Boomerang Burdens: Back to the Nest," Vol. 1 No. 3, Summer 2008.

9  *Forbes*, "The Biggest Market Losers: The Boomers," May 14, 2009.

10  *USA Today*, "Becoming 'parent of your parent' an emotionally wrenching process," June 24, 2007.

11  AARP, "Exclusive AARP Bulletin Poll Reveals New Trends in Multigenerational Housing," March 3, 2009.

12  Heath, Chip, and Amos Tversky, "Preference and Belief: Ambiguity and Competence in Choice under Uncertainty," *Journal of Risk and Uncertainty*, 1991.

13  Benartzi, Shlomo, and Richard H. Thaler, National Bureau of Economic Research, "Heuristics and Biases in Retirement Savings Behavior," 2007.

14  *Science Direct*, "Information friction and investor home bias: A perspective on the effect of global IFRS adoption on the extent of equity home bias," October 30, 2008.

15  Internal Revenue Service, Publication 950 – Introduction to Estate and Gift Taxes, December 2009.

16  National Opinion Research Center at the University of Chicago, "Social comparisons and health: can having richer friends and neighbors make you sick?" June 8, 2009.

17  National Opinion Research Center at the University of Chicago, "Social comparisons and health: can having richer friends and neighbors make you sick?" June 8, 2009.

18  MSN Money, "How does your debt compare?" 2009.

19  Transform Your Money, Money Jokes, Financial Jokes and Funny Stories, 2009.

20  CNN Money, "It's time to unspoil your kids," June 1, 2009.

21  Pew Research Center's Social & Demographic Trends, "Recession Brings Many Young Adults Back to the Nest," November 24, 2009.

# 6

## The Tax Man Will NOT Come Knocking

**TAXADERMY:** [*tak*-sah-dur-mee]

The painful process of being taxed to death by the government. *George and his wife packed up and moved from California to Texas to avoid taxadermy.*

There's an urban legend about someone who takes a job and forgoes a regular paycheck in exchange for receiving a penny at the end of his first day of work and having it double each day for 31 days. Most of us would immediately think with the right side of our brains, and the emotional charge from this intuitive side would say, *"A penny? No way! I'll take the regular paycheck."* Those who took a moment and pulled from the other side of the brain, pausing for reflection, would be rewarded. That's because that penny doubling every day for a month grows to $10,737,418. That's just one example of the power of compounding, which Albert Einstein described as the most powerful force in the universe. What's more incredible is that halfway though the month, on Day 16, the penny is only worth $327. But given time, compounding can be your best friend. Unfortunately, there is a twist to this story. Everyone must pay taxes. That same penny taxed at a 28% tax rate loses its amazing growth because taxes eat away at the compounding. How much do taxes hurt? Well, if you lose 28% of that growth every day it doubles, the penny grows to only $116,373. That's not bad money, but it's a pittance relative to the $10 million plus there would be without taxes. It is also a factor to keep in mind when considering a tax-deferred retirement vehicle or tax-free Roth IRA.

No investment is going to double every day like the Magic Penny. In the world of finance, many professionals utilize a mathematical formula called the Rule of 72, and it provides a thumbnail estimate of how long it may take an investor's portfolio to double in value. The Rule of 72 simply divides 72 by the assumed rate of return to get a rough estimate of how many years it will take for the initial investment to double. For example, if we assume a rate of return of 7.2%, your money will double every 10 years. (Using this rule, at a 10% rate of return, your money would double in 7.2 years.) Simple as that. However, when you apply the reality of taxation, the formula can change dramatically. The Rule of 72 becomes a concept I call 72/33/50; assuming a 33% tax rate, it takes 50% longer to double your money. Sticking with a 7.2% rate of return, net of 33% taxes, it will take 15 years to double your money. Obviously, if you make any changes to these assumptions, the outcome will differ.

There are three Retirementology lessons here: 1) Understand the power of compounding for better and for worse; 2) Don't underestimate the importance of managing taxes, and 3) After the tax man comes knocking, you may need a new door—in other words, the importance of tax planning with regard to your overall planning has been ratcheted up several levels.

# No, The Tax Man Will NOT Come Knocking...He Will Kick the Door Down

The largest annual budget in United States history to date—$3.5 trillion—was passed in early 2009. On top of that, a $787 billion "stimulus" package was signed by the president in February 2009, featuring $4.19 billion for "neighborhood stabilization projects," (which is not money for neighborhoods on a fault line),[1] $10 million to inspect canals in urban areas, and $160 million for "paid volunteers" at the Corporation for National and Community Service.[2] Of course, that was just months after the dubious $700 billion Troubled Asset Relief Program (TARP) passed through Congress at what seemed like the speed of light. TARP was ostensibly designed to rid the financial system of the toxic subprime mortgage-backed securities made possible by government mandate.[3] But in practice, it has been something quite different.

Where this spending ends is anybody's guess, but that guess may be overly optimistic if it doesn't include a crash that costs the American taxpayers untold sums of money and strikes another blow to the economy. If you add up all the recent spending initiatives from Washington, it would be enough to send every person in the world a check for $1,430.[4] Consider that the median American income is around $50,000 annually, and you understand why this sort of spending might have a bad ending for everyone. The new surge in federal government spending is nothing new; it's just the latest in a long tradition of spending in Washington that is unsustainable. For decades before the financial meltdown, politicians and many Americans were doing their best to keep their heads planted firmly in the sand regarding such programs as Medicaid, which is administered by individual states, as well as Medicare and Social Security, which fall under the purview of the federal government. With regard to the two federal programs, America has the equivalent of a $49T mortgage[5] hanging over our heads. With the additional programs and spending, we're adding an additional $9.7T to the deficit.[6]

According to a 2009 Gallup Poll, Americans think that the government wastes 50 cents out of each tax dollar.[7] It's no wonder when you consider some of the ways our tax dollars are being spent. For example, let's look at the $1.15 million it will take to install a guardrail along Oklahoma's Optima Lake.[8] Now, that guardrail might be needed and it might not be; pictures show an existing guardrail that seems to be in perfectly good shape.[9] Of course, that guardrail is surrounding a very big, very shallow, very dry patch of land. It turns out that Optima Lake is, in reality, a reservoir that was built in the 1960s and has never been filled to more than 5% of capacity.[10] A dam and adjacent state park were built alongside the "lake," as were campgrounds, recreational and picnic areas, and a boat ramp for a lake that *"loses 100% of its inflowing water to evaporation,"* according to The Geological Society of America.[11] Optima Lake, claimed Alan Riffel, city manager of nearby Woodward, Oklahoma, in 1997, is *"one of Oklahoma's greatest boondoggles."*[12]

So why does one of Oklahoma's greatest boondoggles have to become a boondoggle for the rest of the country? Why does $1.15 million of federal money have to go to a singular state's road project that may not even be necessary? If a new guardrail is really necessary, does it really cost $1.15 million? What's wrong with the present guardrail? What about a toll for the people driving on the road that surrounds Optima Lake? Are there other millions of federal dollars being proposed for other states' dubious projects?

The proposals and ideas coming out of the nation's capitol today reveal that this trend is going to continue. Key congressional committees released a proposal in mid-July of 2009 to impose a "surtax" on income earned above certain levels. If this proposal were to become law, there would be a 1–2% tax increase for couples earning between $350,000 and $500,000. Those taxes would go up to 5.4% on families earning more than $1,000,000.[13] Speaking of couples earning seven figures, they'd also get hit with a 5% "millionaire's tax." Senate leaders are also floating the idea of applying the 1.45% Medicare tax, which presently hits only "earned" income like wages, to capital gains and dividends.[14] On top of that, there's a proposal to reduce the itemized deduction rate for families with incomes over $250,000 from as much as 35% to 28%, costing approximately $70 for every $1,000 in mortgage interest deductions.[15]

Granted, as of this writing, all these taxes have merely been proposed. If passed, they could have a big effect on how business is conducted in the United States. Many small business owners, the economic engine of our economy, take in seven figures in gross income and then accept a majority of their personal pay as business dividends, for instance. How will these proposals affect the small businessperson in America? It's anybody's guess.

America is now at the point where we have more debt than was ever created by our first 43 presidents and 110 Congresses—combined. Interest payments alone on the government stimulus package will amount to an estimated $347 billion.[16] That will bring the "stimulus" bill itself to nearly $1.2 trillion.[17] On a grander scale, domestic discretionary spending (that includes "stimulus" funds) has been raised 80% over 2008 levels, bringing Washington's budget to 12.3% of GDP—by a staggering margin, the biggest percentage of

GDP since World War II. In the meantime, publicly held national debt will also double to more than $15 trillion.[18] All this spending is on top of future federal obligations that have risen to more than $50 trillion.[19]

Even before the meltdown, taxes were a threat to your retirement. Because those with the most money are taxed at a higher rate, 1% of American families ended up paying 40% of America's personal taxes.[20] The families in the rest of the top 5% had family incomes of $160,000 to $410,000 and paid another 20% of the total personal income taxes that were paid nationwide.[21]

## After the Meltdown, Taxes Are Your Retirement Catastrophe

Higher federal income tax rates are likely going to be reintroduced to the public on January 1, 2011[22] and will impact many aspects of a person's financial plan. Investors are already adjusting to it by pulling taxable income from their investments now and planning to leave their investments where they are after the higher capital gains taxes take effect. In the meantime, ever higher state taxes in places such as New York, New Jersey, and California have served to foreshadow the problems that higher taxes cause.

- Higher rates will immediately keep more dollars from circulating in the private sector.[23]
- Higher tax rates may cause an expansion of government programs, spending, and debt if the higher tax rates fail to result in higher tax receipts,[24] which are the tax revenues received by government from all sources: the sum of personal current taxes, taxes on production and imports, taxes on corporate income, and taxes from the rest of the world.
- Who's going to pay for it...especially after the Chinese stop buying our debt?[25]
- Although the Alternative Minimum Tax (AMT) was in place prior to the meltdown, year after year, Congress "punts" this issue by simply changing some of the criteria, instead of eliminating it.[26] AMT ensnares millions of Americans, costing them

each thousands of dollars in taxes that they wouldn't pay if they didn't fall into the AMT net.

- In spite of all the talk about a flat tax, or elimination of an income tax in favor of a national Value Added Tax (VAT), it seems our present tax code—all 60,000+ pages of it—is here to stay.

# Hidden Taxes—Come Out, Come Out, Wherever You Are

Taxes hit some people harder than others. But make no mistake: They hit everyone, in spite of the fact that right now, in 2009, 43.4% of the American population doesn't pay any federal income tax.[27] Some of these people even receive money from the feds, according to a study published on April 14, 2009, by the Tax Center Policy, a joint project of the Urban Institute and the Brookings Institution.[28] So a total of 65.6 million Americans aren't directly affected at all by the threat of income tax increases or the increases we know are likely coming in 2011 when the 2001 and 2003 tax cuts are set to expire.[29]

So who are these fortunate people who pay no federal income taxes? Basically, they're the people who earn around $35,000 a year. They're not rich, but they do get a tax break. Or do they? A recent poll revealed that more than half of American cigarette smokers earn less than $36,000 per year, which means it's this group that pays the $1.01 federal excise (another euphemism) tax on every pack of cigarettes sold within the United States—a tax that was greatly increased just this year.[30] Many states also collect handsomely when a citizen decides to light up. That's a tax increase on lower income Americans, no matter how you look at it. We pay taxes on just about every good, every service, and every single thing we buy, and many of those taxes are often overlooked. Take a look at your utility bills, or that hotel bill that is slid under the door at checkout time. The typical cell phone bill is also an interesting case. A closer look at the breakdown of charges reveals that the actual cost of making calls and taking calls is a fraction of the total. Much of the total is supplemented by the

Regulatory Cost Recovery Charge, the federal and state Universal Connectivity Charges, the City Special Purpose District Tax, and myriad other tax levies. If you are collecting Social Security benefits, you may not be aware of a hidden tax that may be cutting into your retirement income. Did you know there is the potential of having up to 85% of your Social Security benefits taxed?[31] The overriding problem with this tax is that income from all sources is counted, including wages, earned interest, rental income, dividends, and tax-exempt income from certain investment vehicles. The Social Security tax kicks in at $25,000 ($32,000 for couples).[32]

Some taxes are completely hidden from sight. Sure, there are states and municipalities that refuse to charge a sales tax on food and clothing, but think of all the taxes that are built into the price and passed on to the end user: A rancher pays taxes just to set up and do business; when he sells his cattle, he collects taxes on the transaction; the slaughterhouse that buys the cattle pays taxes just to do business and then collects taxes on the transaction to the grocery store. All these businesses pay taxes when they purchase supplies—though they sometimes get tax breaks on these items—as well as when they pay the rent or mortgage on the place where they conduct their business. The percentage of the price of that hamburger you put on your grill that's charged simply to pay taxes is astounding. It's also something of which very few people are aware.

## Does the Taxman Own a Moving Van?

Taxes have the power to drive behavior. Consider what's happened in New York and New Jersey over a period of ten years. A June 26, 2009 *The Wall Street Journal* article titled "The Albany-Trenton-Sacramento Disease" highlighted that between 1999 and 2009, New York was the unrivaled king of the financial world and that New Jersey was the union's third wealthiest state behind Connecticut and Massachusetts.[33] Where are they now? Both states are teetering on bankruptcy. Why? Excessive government spending is the chief cause; just look at the $65 million New York is spending on teachers who aren't teaching.[34] Not surprisingly, politicians in these states spent the past number of years paying for their spending with a "tax the wealthy" policy. The state/local income tax burden in New York is the highest in the nation, perhaps the reason why more than 1.5 million people, along with their earning revenue, have left the state (1.1 million from New York City) in the last decade.[35] The top five property tax counties in the United States call New Jersey and New York home.[36] From 1998 to 2007, New York and New Jersey have ranked 36th and 31st, respectively, in job creation despite a booming national economy during much of that span.[37] Why is that? Could the reason be that New Yorkers bear the highest income tax burden in the country?[38] Could it be that the people of New Jersey bear the sixth highest income tax burden?[39] Could part of the reason also be that so many people were leaving these two states specifically because of taxes and settling in more tax-friendly locales?[40]

Take the case of longtime Rochester, New York, billionaire Tom Golisano. Mr. Golisano has a long and involved history in the state, including three gubernatorial runs. But he announced in 2009 that, at the age of 67, he's moving his full-time residence to Naples, Florida. He claims the move will save him $13,000 a day in state taxes, as the Sunshine State has no state income tax, and he may even be considering a run for a Florida senate seat. Of course, as owner of the National Hockey League franchise in Buffalo, the Sabres, he may still be paying the state's onerous business taxes for some time.[41] Tom Golisano is just one of many people who have left New York and New Jersey recently as part of a quest for lower taxes and a better opportunity to spend the money for which they work in a way that they see fit. That's why New York ranks first and New Jersey ranks third in the nation for "moving vans leaving the state." So which state is second?

## Pillaging the Golden State

For millions, California is more than a state; it is a state of mind. Geographically, there's nothing like it, with many distinct regions and climates. The central valley possesses some of the richest farming soil in the world; the temperate coast is home to numerous vineyards and much of the state's population. Its history is as unique and diverse as any state in the country. Over the past 500 years, parts of California have flown the flags of Russia, Spain, Mexico, and finally, the United States.[42]

In recent decades, California has been more than home to Hollywood and the entertainment industry; it's been an impressive entrepreneurial and shipping hub. Arguably, California has been an incubator for great societal and business ideas. Perhaps that's why the old saying, *"As California goes, so goes the nation,"* rings so true. The wealth that's been developed in California could have been foretold by the fact that the first great American migration to the state was initiated by people going there to discover gold. For years after that, California was indeed the place to go if you wanted to hit the big time.

But today, California is a different story altogether. Sure, the state still produces some of the world's best wine. Hewlett-Packard and Apple Computer, companies started by young men in California garages, still call the state home.[43] The $1.8 trillion economy is still larger than Russia's and represents the world's eighth-largest economy.[44] California is still the most populous state in the country.[45] But the mood for business and the prospects for the citizens in the state are pretty dim.

For approximately eight consecutive years, from April 2000 to July 2008, more people have moved out of California than have moved in, to the tune of almost 1.4 million.[46] Only New York's tax structure has made more people leave.[47] Companies are exiting the Golden State in record numbers and taking their employees with them. The people left behind are hurting, as the state's unemployment rate was 12.3% in October 2009, the highest level since records started being kept.[48] Every day we're hearing stories about how movies are being shot in places other than California. And what's prompting these studios to make these moves? For the same reason that I believe California's entire economy is tanking: taxes.

Against the backdrop of a state government in Sacramento that's so inept the state's debts are mounting at a rate of $1.7 million per day, taxes have kept going up to the point where California features the highest state tax (10.3%) on million-dollar income earners and the lowest tax (1%) on low-income earners.[49] For the 2010 fiscal year that began July 1, 2009, there is a $142 billion states' revenue shortfall and that's causing states—including California, New York, and New Jersey—to raise incomes taxes, gas, sales or estate taxes which will encourage more top wage earners to flee those states.[50] With the tax burden so heavy on people who are leaving the state, is it any surprise that California started issuing IOUs instead of checks to creditors on July 1, 2009[51] or that the state's deficit in 2010 is projected to be $33.9 billion?[52] On top of that, California's home prices average around $300,000, in spite of a 34.5% drop in 2008, so the cost of owning or renting in California continues to plague the state.[53]

In the meantime, the tax-friendly state of Texas added more jobs (and thereby a bigger tax base) than California and all the other states combined during 2008.[54] So what did California politicians do in the spring of 2009? They asked the voters for more tax money via ballot initiative. As window dressing, they put a "spending cap" on the ballot, which the voters saw through as a ruse. The voters rejected everything. The ATM is closed, they said. All the piggy banks have been raided. There's no more money for the politicians to spend, and California is on the verge of bankruptcy, with a $24 billion budget deficit.[55] The state's credit rating is the worst of the 50 states, and Sacramento's $59 billion general obligation bonds are on a negative credit watch.[56]

California politicians have long framed the tax issue as a "pay-higher-taxes-or-we're-going-to-lay-off-teachers" type of debate. But perhaps the state's citizens have gotten wise that they're not getting very good value out of their education tax dollars in particular and may feel like laying off teachers would be a good idea. Right now, California already has the highest paid classroom teachers in the country, but their students have the second lowest test scores.[57] Proposition 1B would have furnished the state's schools with $9 billion more, with one argument being that schools need more money for more teachers.[58] But according to California gubernatorial candidate and former eBay Chair Meg Whitman, 50% of the state's education budget goes into overhead, not classrooms. (Connecticut, conversely, commits 20% to overhead.)[59] So where would half of the proposed $9 billion really go? That's anyone's guess, so it's certainly good that California's citizens have decided to turn off the spigot of tax dollars going to Sacramento. *"As California goes, so goes the nation?"* Let's hope not.

# Are There Bell Bottoms in Our Future?

Many people are comparing the climate of the 2000s to that of the mid- to late '70s. There may be a lot of merit to that argument. As a country, we're increasing the money supply; pledging heavy government spending on industries and technologies that haven't been able to survive on their own merit; relying too heavily on hostile countries for our energy needs when those needs could easily be fulfilled by our own resources; and discouraging risk capital from being invested. The only thing that seems to separate us from the '70s is a prevalence of bell bottoms, feathered hair, and disco music.

What we do have now, however, that we didn't have then is a recent memory of the greatest economic expansion in the history of mankind. Starting in the early 1980s, the American economy experienced almost monthly growth, new businesses and industries were born, and job creation became so robust that we experienced long spells of "full employment." Things weren't always rosy, but it was a long enough stretch that there are people in the workforce right now who are experiencing their first recession in a lifetime, presuming that an ever-expanding economy was their birthright. A big reason for that is because many currently affected by today's meltdown weren't alive in 1944–45 when workers who earned more than $200,000 were taxed at an amazing 94% or in 1951–63 when top earners making more than $400,000 were taxed at 91%.[60] Though the 1950s were a time of economic expansion in the United States, there were so few people affected by the 91% tax rates (and there were so many tax shelters available in the pages of the IRS tax code) that no one allowed his cash income to come anywhere close to the highest rate.

Chances are that the immediate future will be economically turbulent if you're of any means at all. The dollar is getting weaker versus foreign currencies and with the Federal Reserve printing money to buy government bonds, foreigners are leery that the American debt might just be inflated away.[61] June 18, 2009 brought the announcement of a record issuance of $104 billion in U.S. government bonds and the worry intensified that interest rates would have to go up to entice people to buy up all the paper.[62] In investing circles, you're often told, *"The trend is your friend."* That's not the case here. The top 20% of households paid 81.2% of all taxes during the presidency of

Bill Clinton, and in 2006, these households paid a record 86.3% of all taxes.[63] And that trend is only going to continue since, according to President Obama's 2010 federal budget, increased taxes on "the rich" will equal 0.3% of GDP—echoes of Herbert Hoover's tax hikes that put the "Great" into "Great Depression."[64] Or of California today.

What about the wealthy? Presently, the goal in Washington is to take people who earn $250,000 a year or more in income, approximately 2.6 million Americans, and collect $636.7 billion in taxes from them.[65] Additionally, "carried interest" from a hedge fund, a venture capital firm, a private equity firm, or some other partnership presently taxed at 15% may soon be taxed at 39.6%.[66] In 1984, a tax on retirees' Social Security benefits was introduced, which made up to 50% of a beneficiary's Social Security check taxable if the person's other income—retirement plan payout, investment income, and so on—exceeded $25,000 annually ($32,000 for couples). Back then, that tax hit about 10% of retirees; in 2009, it hit one-third, and in 2018, it's projected to hit 45%.[67]

The Social Security "payroll" tax is the only regressive tax in the American system, which means the federal government stops collecting it past a certain threshold of income (in 2009, it was up to $102,000, according to the Social Security website). Early in the 2008 presidential campaign, President Obama wrote an op-ed in Iowa's *Quad City Times* on September 21, 2007, that read, "*If we kept the payroll tax rate exactly the same but applied it to all earnings and not just the first $97,000, we could eliminate the entire Social Security shortfall.*" Social Security, along with Medicare and Medicaid, have gotten so big they now take up 8% of GDP (Gross Domestic Product).[68] In 2050, these programs are expected to balloon to 18.6% of GDP.[69]

Presently, the tax code (there it is again) dictates that the portion of healthcare benefits that are paid by employers is not considered income and is not subject to taxation. If that changes, I would guess that people might have extra "income" on which they'll have to pay taxes. Then there are multinational corporations: The administration recently called for the money that American multinationals earn overseas and keep overseas (and is already taxed overseas) to be taxed the same way it would be taxed if it were earned here at home. Currently, the law calls for that money to be taxed only after it is "repatriated" to the United States.[70]

We also know that the top federal income tax rate is scheduled to go from 35% to 39.6% along with many other rates in 2011. On top of that, capital gains taxes will likely increase from 15% to 20% for Americans who are in the 28% income tax bracket ($82,850 gross annually and up for a single taxpayer) or higher.[71] What will be the effect? The Heritage Foundation insists that these rising capital gains taxes will only serve to promote a "lock-in effect," where investors simply keep invested money where it is to avoid taxes.[72] It also means that the government will have to go somewhere else to get money. Be ready.

# The Retirement Brain Game

**Mental Accounting**—Money does not come with labels; people put labels on their money. People assign different purposes for different amounts of money. They'll keep cash in a low-interest savings account for one purpose while borrowing money at a higher rate for another, thus losing money overall. The brain makes accounts for different purposes; for instance, the savings account could be going toward a television whereas the borrowed money could go toward a car.

As one of those certainties in life, taxes never sleep, nor do they retire. But before you can manage them, you may need to perceive taxes differently than you do now. In Chapter 2, "Gold Dust on Sushi," we explored how *mental accounting* affects our spending and saving behavior. This behavior can also be used to illustrate the way many of us view taxes.

For example: *How much did you earn last year?* What is your first answer?

Now, is the number that came to mind gross or net of taxes? Remember, the question was how much did you earn last year, not how much did you keep after the government took its share. More often than not, we account for our annual salary without considering taxes. In short, our system of mental accounting typically leads us to discount the impact of taxes on our lives. And it is precisely this type of *mental accounting* error that can cloud our decisions when it comes to retirement planning.

| Transparent | Opaque | Takeaway |
|---|---|---|
| *Gross Pay* | *Net Pay* | |
| $50,000 | $36,000 (Assumes hypothetical 28% tax rate.) | Basing budgets on your gross rather than net salary can lead to overspending and underpreparing. |

The reasonable follow-up question would be, *"Is that before or after taxes?"* Many of us have no idea how much we really bring home every year; we simply treat our gross income like it's penalty free and don't account for the bite that taxes take out of every dollar.

How about this question: *"How much did you pay in taxes last year?"*

You'd be shocked at the number of people who respond, *"Nothing! I got a refund!"*

Many people have no idea that they give the government a tax-free loan by overpaying their taxes, because they receive a refund. By calculating deductions more carefully, that refund money could have been theirs all along—being invested or earning interest and adding to their retirement accounts.

To put the total tax bite into perspective, note that on average, you spend more time working to pay your taxes than you will spend working for food, clothing, and shelter combined, as shown in Figure 6.1.

The opaque nature of taxes, along with inflation, can also have a devastating effect on your long-term retirement plan.

The point is, managing taxes is a key component to retirement planning, and the sooner you adjust your thinking to address taxes, the better you can deal with their impact. Don't look now, but taxes are everywhere. As discussed earlier, the opaque nature of taxes can hurt us, but even their transparency can confuse us, and certainly polarize us as a society. In general, people react to taxes depending on how they see themselves in the context of the tax and their own individual behavior. When people see themselves as part of a group doing something together, they can look upon a certain tax as a civic virtue.[73]

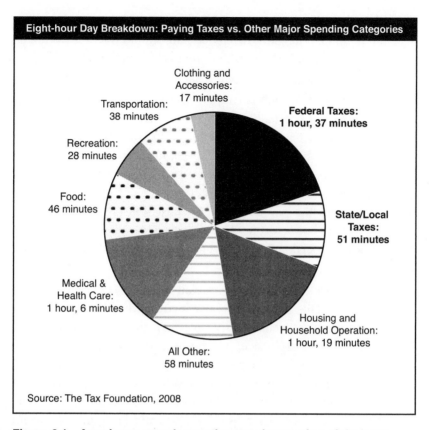

**Figure 6.1    Americans spend more than two hours of an eight-hour workday paying taxes.**

Take an experience that happens with regularity across the country: the "stadium debate." Just about every city in the United States has had a professional football, baseball, or basketball team threaten to leave if a new stadium is not built for them. In response, many city and state governments devise tax schemes (and often direct giveaways to team owners) to keep the team in town and give people a sense of civic pride. One tactic is that a sales tax of an extra cent per $10 (or a similar sum) is proposed in an area in the immediate vicinity of the stadium. Fans of the team, even those individuals who normally are very much against additional taxes, see that their tax dollars are going toward something they value and reason with themselves that there is a positive civic virtue to seeing the tax take effect—especially since the tax can be avoided by people who don't support it.

The other side is made up of people who reason that the old stadium suits the team just fine and the city or state should not be subsidizing playpens for millionaire players and their billionaire owners.

When this sort of debate takes place, the tax becomes the biggest bone of contention, which is strange when you consider how minuscule the proposed tax really is compared to so many other taxes we pay. But it does set entire societies up into two distinct camps, or social categories, rather than as a group of individuals. This appeal to civic virtue—whether it's for the team staying and playing in a new building or the belief that tax money should not go to such businesses—changes the psychology of the situation in which the tax is proposed. That's because it puts individuals into wider, more inclusive categories in a social context in which they wouldn't otherwise find themselves.[74]

Property taxes are, in theory, meant to go toward funding local school systems. This gives school boards cover when it comes time to raise property taxes because they can claim that educational needs have become more expensive and the increase—known in my community as a "mill levy"—is necessary. Once again, this tax puts people into groups and pits them against one another. Some people have kids in the local schools, and they feel passionate about the need for the property tax increases, whereas others may not have kids at all and wonder why it's incumbent on them to provide for other peoples' children. Still others may have children in private schools, in schools for children with special needs, or children away at college—all of which are expenses added on top of the local property tax. No matter what sort of stance a person takes individually on taxes, the psychology changes when a locality is involved and people put themselves in groups that are either for or against the increase.

# Improve Your Retirementology IQ

Because taxes permeate every transaction, it's difficult to avoid the Tax Man. Sure, you can buy a less expensive car, house, or cup of coffee, but you're still going to pay taxes on them. Government officials have always spent taxpayers' money freely, and that's not going to change anytime soon. The key to controlling the impact of taxes is to develop a bit of selfishness about the money you work so hard to earn. It's yours, after all.

## Understand Your Tax Position

When it comes to managing taxes, what worked just a couple years ago may not work anymore. Whereas you once simply expected your money to grow every time you opened up your retirement account statements, now you're probably just hoping you haven't lost any more. One way you can avoid giving too much to the Tax Man is by taking advantage of what is referred to as tax harvesting. Consider that *taxes are the single highest cost you'll bear as an investor*: Short-term capital gains rates can be taxed at combined state and federal rates of 40% or more, and long-term capital gains taxes can total 20% or more. Those rates are likely to increase, which means that if you have seen your portfolio appreciate over the long run, you might be advised to sell some of your holdings now to lock in their gains and enjoy the relatively low tax rates. Of course, the past 24 months or so have seen the value of investments drop severely, only to recover quite a bit during the summer of 2009. That means you could very likely also own short-term securities that are worth a lot less now than they were when they were acquired. How to make the most of the situation? Tax harvesting.

Tax harvesting is a strategy that enables an investor to offset capital gains with losses, and vice versa, thus potentially minimizing the tax impact. In consultation with a qualified tax adviser, some investors may be able to sell securities that have dropped in value—in other words, *harvest* these losses and use these losses to offset gains that have been realized. Or, they can realize gains in their account to offset losses from other investments. The goal is to balance one's portfolio's gains and losses for the year to potentially minimize the tax impact. Capital losses generated for tax purposes can also extend beyond capital gains. The tax law generally allows an investor to realize up to $3,000 in capital losses to be deducted from ordinary income each year. For an investor in the 35% federal income tax bracket, a $3,000 loss could reduce his or her federal tax bill by $1,050. Harvesting investment losses may be an option for reducing an annual tax bill.

Before moving forward, you should run the numbers with your adviser. Basically, what you may want to do is figure out how much of your appreciated assets you'd like to sell and determine the taxes on that. Then determine how many of your more recently acquired securities can be sold at a loss, thereby offsetting the taxes incurred on the appreciated investments. Tax harvesting is a great way to take advantage of investments that turn sour and help you realize the gains that your good investment choices have earned for you. Yet many investors with taxable accounts fail to take full advantage of their losses in such a way.

Think ahead—not just to your retirement, but also beyond. Do you know how to pass assets on to your heirs without having them incur huge tax burdens? Do you have any charities to which you'd also like to leave money? Speak to an adviser regarding tax ramifications and the taxes that will be due and payable by the recipients. Estate planning for your surviving spouse and children can be vital to their ongoing financial health, so establish a basic estate plan and standard trusts like a living trust, a credit shelter trust, and a bypass trust. Taking care of these things can make the difference between seeing millions go to your family—or to the IRS. Procrastinating—staying where you've been and not adjusting your portfolio—can be very expensive given the changing landscape. Many people have trouble with the basics, like filing their tax return on time every year. The IRS estimates that 10.3 million individuals will apply for a six-month extension in 2009, out of almost 140 million individual Form 1040 filers. The more you procrastinate, the more you can fall behind. The outlook has changed dramatically over the past 12, 24, 36 months. You have to change with it. Have your adviser give you a top-to-bottom review of your investments and be open to moving assets to instruments that have tax advantages, as well as prospects for growth. Ask as many questions as you can think of and be open to ideas and strategies you may never have considered in the past.

### Monitor the Legislative Process

In the Internet age, it's remarkably easy to track the progress of legislation as it moves from Congressional committees to the House and Senate floors and, ultimately, the president's desk. A surfeit of commentary, analyses, and posturing will surely be evident in all media channels. It may be best to focus on professional, nonpartisan sources, such as the American Institute of Certified Public Accountants or the Tax Policy Center. It's long been said that knowledge is power; in this case, early knowledge can mean even more power. And lower taxes.

### Understand Your Goals

You may have goals now that you didn't have five years ago. You may have goals five years from now that you don't have today. Make sure you and your adviser both have a clear understanding of those goals at all times. When a goal changes, contact your adviser and talk about how best to reach that goal. Of course, this relationship with your adviser is also a two-way street, so be sure that she updates you on any changes in tax laws that could hinder or enhance your ability to meet your goals, such as the way the Tax Increase Protection and Reconciliation Act of 2006 (TIPRA) affected Roth IRAs. Go back three decades and you'll see a perfect example of the importance of this communication: When the 401(k) plan was created and came into effect, the retirement investing landscape changed dramatically. People who acted on that development right away built retirement wealth much more quickly.

Also, be sure to understand your goals after you've retired. Know what your sources of income will be, ranging from pensions to Social Security to investments, and make sure you have a plan that can provide money for your entire lifetime. Work with an adviser to help you take a solid aim at your retirement dreams.

### Run the Numbers

When evaluating alternative courses of action, there is no substitute for running the numbers. Your adviser or accountant can run a side-by-side projection of the expected tax result. This is commonly used to evaluate the potential benefit of one tax strategy over another. Projections should be updated frequently using current data and reliable estimates. Trying to predict the outcome of a particular strategy without running the numbers may be problematic. Historically, many people didn't run numbers because the tax consequences were more of an annoyance than a major penalty. This is changing in a number of areas, and it makes sense to become accustomed to this drill.

### The Time Might Be Right to Convert to a Roth IRA

Converting assets from a traditional IRA to a Roth IRA allows an investor to pay taxes today and receive tax-free income in the future. Additionally, Roth IRAs are not subject to required minimum distributions (RMDs), so an investor who does not need income can allow their legacy to continue growing and pass income tax free to heirs. Roth conversions have been available since the introduction of Roth IRAs over a decade ago, but significant tax policy changes in 2010 may result in a surge of popularity for this tax strategy.

With the nation facing unprecedented financial challenges, the tax-hedge and tax-diversification advantage of Roth IRAs and future tax-free income may be particularly appealing. If you think income tax rates will rise in the future, paying taxes now to receive tax-free income in the future is worth consideration. By working with an adviser or using the Roth income calculator on a financial planning website, you can measure the impact on your net income in retirement with and without a Roth conversion.

### Harness the Power of Tax Deferral

Taxes do not need to be an obstacle on your journey to asset growth. You can delay the impact of taxes by considering the use of tax-deferred retirement account vehicles. In a taxable vehicle, you pay taxes on your earnings each year. But, in a tax-deferred vehicle, your money grows free of taxes until you withdraw it. In any tax environment, it makes good economic sense to delay taxation until the money is needed. Tax-deferred vehicles keep your principal and earnings, including money that would otherwise be diverted to pay taxes, working for you.

Consider the hypothetical examples in Figure 6.2, comparing currently taxable growth versus tax-deferred growth of $100,000, assuming an 8% annual rate of return and a 28% federal tax rate over a 30-year period. The $100,000 still earns more than it would without tax deferral.

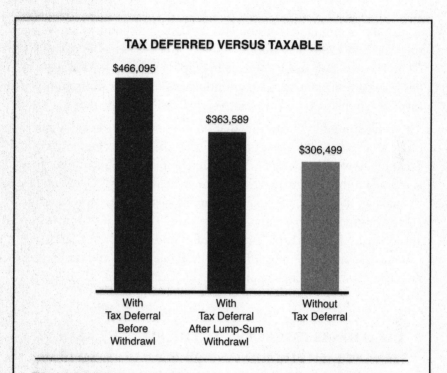

**TAX DEFERRED VERSUS TAXABLE**

$466,095

$363,589

$306,499

With Tax Deferral Before Withdrawl

With Tax Deferral After Lump-Sum Withdrawl

Without Tax Deferral

This chart is hypothetical and for illustrative purposes only. The hypothetical rates of return shown in this chart are not guaranteed and should not be viewed as indicative of the past or future performance of any particular investment or product. This chart is based on a hypothetical situation assuming taxable and tax-deferred growth of an initial $100,000 investment, an 8% annual rate of return, and a 28% tax rate over a 20-year period. No additional investments were made over this time period. Chart does not reflect any fees and charges associated with investment products. If these changes were reflected, the results would be lower.

Changes in tax rates and tax treatment of investment earnings may impact the hypothetical example above. Lower maximum tax rates on capital gains and dividends would increase the results shown. Investors should consider their individual investment time horizon and income tax brackets, both current and anticipated, when making an investment decision. Please note that there would be tax penalties for early withdrawal, along with other potential fees and charges.

**Figure 6.2   The power of tax deferral**

Complaining about taxes is as American as apple pie. Americans have a long history of avoiding them, evading them, deferring them, and throwing tea into a harbor as a way of protesting them. The only thing we don't seem to be good at regarding taxes, besides lowering them, is minimizing their impact on our overall financial well-being. Taking advantage of the many tax deductions that may be available to you is imperative if you hope to maximize the money you could have available in retirement. But the IRS isn't going to notify you to make sure you take them all…that's the job of a knowledgeable adviser or CPA. These people are invaluable in helping you reach your goals by designing a retirement plan distribution schedule that starts after you turn 59½ so that you don't run into early distribution penalties.

As illustrated by the penny that doubles every day in value but is taxed at a rate of 28% every day, taxes diminish a person's ability to accumulate wealth. The fact that so much of the tax intake right now is morally dubious only makes it more difficult to pay taxes. The key to making the most of your retirement accounts in the years to come—no matter what happens with taxes—is to lower your exposure to taxes at every turn. Tax deferral is one of the best friends you can have, so make the most of what's available to you and watch your nest egg grow without the constraint that taxes would otherwise put on it.

**TAXATION IS EMERGING AS THE SINGLE LARGEST FINANCIAL CHALLENGE FOR BOOMERS, SO IT IS IMPORTANT TO FACTOR THE IMPACT OF TAXES INTO RETIREMENT PLANNING.**[75]

# Endnotes

1  Fox News, "Republicans Object to Stimulus Dollars for ACORN," January 27, 2009.

2  iRreport.com, "Pork: Obama's 'Stimulus' Package," February 7, 2009.

3  *The Washington Post*, "Restore TARP to Its First Purpose," November 26, 2008.

4  Bloomberg, "U.S. Taxpayers Risk $9.7 Trillion on Bailout Programs (Update1)," February 9, 2009.

5　MyBudget360.com, "American Debtor Psycho: $49 Trillion in Debt. The Real Reason why the Credit Crisis is Bigger than You Think," October 19, 2008.

6　Bloomberg, "U.S. Taxpayers Risk $9.7 Trillion on Bailout Programs (Update1)," February 9, 2009.

7　Gallup, "Americans: Uncle Sam Wastes 50 Cents on the Dollar," September 15, 2009.

8　*The Washington Times*, "Senator says billions wasted on stimulus," June 16, 2009.

9　Oklahoma City News 9, "Senator: Oklahoma Stimulus Project Wasteful," June 4, 2009.

10　Science Direct, "Doomed reservoirs in Kansas, USA? Climate change and groundwater mining on the Great Plains lead to unsustainable surface water storage," August 3, 2007.

11　The Geological Society of America, "Droughts and Reservoirs: Finding Storage Space Underground," September 18, 2006.

12　Enid News, "Water Puzzle: Aquifer's uncertain future has city making other plans," November 28, 2007.

13　CNN Money, "Tax the rich to pay for…everything?" July 15, 2009.

14　CNN Money, "Tax the rich to pay for…everything?" July 15, 2009.

15　SF Gate, "Mortgage interest tax deduction cut criticized," February 28, 2009.

16　CNN Money, "Stimulus with interest: $1.2 trillion," January 27, 2009.

17　CNN Money, "Stimulus with interest: $1.2 trillion," January 27, 2009.

18　The Heritage Foundation, *Backgrounder*, "The Obama Budget: Spending, Taxes, and Doubling the National Debt," No. 2249, March 16, 2009.

19　U.S. Government Printing Office, Committee on Homeland Security and Governmental Affairs, "Congress' Role in Federal Financial Management: Is It Efficient, Accountable, and Transparent in the Way It Appropriates Funds?" One Hundred Ninth Congress, Second Session, May 25, 2006.

20　*The Wall Street Journal*, "Tax Withholding Is Bad for Democracy," August 13, 2009.

21　*The Wall Street Journal*, "Tax Withholding Is Bad for Democracy," August 13, 2009.

22　Tax Policy Center: 2010 Budget Tax Proposals, Tax Increases on High-Income Taxpayers, 2009.

23　The Heritage Foundation, *Backgrounder*, "The Obama Budget: Spending, Taxes, and Doubling the National Debt," No. 2249, March 16, 2009.

24　The Heritage Foundation, *Backgrounder*, "The Obama Budget: Spending, Taxes, and Doubling the National Debt," No. 2249, March 16, 2009.

25  Fox News, "What if China Stops Buying U.S. Debt?" February 3, 2009.

26  Tax Foundation, "Special Report: Fixing the Alternative Minimum Tax," No. 155, May 2007.

27  CBS News, "The Income Tax System is Broken," April 15, 2009.

28  CBS News, "The Income Tax System is Broken," April 15, 2009.

29  CBS News, "The Income Tax System is Broken," April 15, 2009.

30  Gallup, "Cigarette Tax Will Affect Low-Income Americans Most," April 1, 2009; CNN, "Smokers feeling abused as federal tax hike hits," April 4, 2009.

31  About.com, Tax Planning, U.S., "Social Security Benefits," December 17, 2008.

32  AARP Bulletin Today, "Recouping 'Lost' Social Security Benefits After Going Back to Work," August 20, 2009

33  *The Wall Street Journal*, "The Albany-Trenton-Sacramento Disease," June 26, 2009.

34  *New York Daily News*, "Teachers in trouble spending years in 'rubber room' limbo that costs $65M," May 4, 2008.

35  *New York Post*, "Tax refugees staging escape from New York," October 27, 2009.

36  *Forbes*, "Who Pays America's Highest Property Taxes?" January 23, 2009.

37  *The Wall Street Journal*, "The Albany-Trenton-Sacramento Disease," June 26, 2009.

38  *The Wall Street Journal*, "The Albany-Trenton-Sacramento Disease," June 26, 2009.

39  *The Wall Street Journal*, "The Albany-Trenton-Sacramento Disease," June 26, 2009.

40  *New York Post*, "Tax refugees staging escape from New York," October 27, 2009.

41  *The Buffalo News*, "Golisano leaving New York to escape income taxes," May 15, 2009.

42  Encyclopedia, History of California to 1899.

43  Apple, Press Info Bios: Steve Jobs, February 2009; Hewlett-Packard, "HP Fast Facts," 2009.

44  Center for Continuing Study of the California Economy, 2008 California Economy Rankings, August 2009.

45  U.S. Census Bureau, State & County QuickFacts: California, November 17, 2009.

46  U.S. Census Bureau, Rank of Net Domestic Migration for State Population Estimates: April 1, 2000 to July 1, 2008, released December 22, 2008.

47  *New York Post*, "Tax refugees staging escape from New York," October 27, 2009.

48  U.S. Bureau of Labor Statistics, California Unemployment Rate, December 10, 2009.

49  *Times*, "California faces financial meltdown as debt grows by $1.7m an hour," December 12, 2008; Center for Continuing Study of the California Economy, "Is California A High Tax State?" October 2007.

50  *Barron's Penta*, "Fleeing the Tax Man," September 28, 2009.

51  *MarketWatch*, "Bank of America to accept California state IOUs," July 1, 2009.

52  *The Wall Street Journal*, "The Albany-Trenton-Sacramento Disease," June 26, 2009.

53  *Los Angeles Times*, "Southern California's median home price drops below $300,000," December 17, 2008.

54  Texas Comptroller of Public Accounts, Texas Annual Cash Report, Fiscal 2008, "Review of the Texas Economy in Fiscal 2008: A Lone Star Among States," 2008.

55  *Reuters*, "California set to issue IOUs as fiscal crisis weighs," June 24, 2009.

56  *Los Angeles Times*, "California's credit rating may get cut further," June 17, 2009.

57  Tough Money Love, "Escaping High Taxes," May 18, 2009.

58  *The Mercury News*, "Educators split on propositions that would create school funding," May 19, 2009.

59  *Pittsburgh Tribune-Review*, "Meg Whitman's suicide-prevention plan," July 5, 2009.

60  National Taxpayers Union, History of Federal Individual Income Bottom and Top Bracket Rates, 1944–45, 1951, 1952–53 and 1954–63.

61  *The Wall Street Journal*, "The Weak-Dollar Threat to Prosperity," October 7, 2009; *The Economist*, "Will world governments cut the real size of their debt through inflation?" June 11, 2009.

62  *Reuters*, "Treasury to Auction $104 Billion In Debt Next Week, a Record," June 18, 2009.

63  *Barrons*, "Redefining 'Wealthy,'" May 18, 2009.

64  Fox News Forum, "Obama's Scary Hoover-Style Tax Hikes," March 2, 2009.

65  *The Sydney Morning Herald*, "'Obama Robin Hood' to tax the rich," February 27, 2009.

66  About.com, Tax Planning: U.S., "Obama's Tax Proposals," May 21, 2009.

67  CNN *Money*, "Stop soaking the not-so-rich," June 2, 2009.

68  The Heritage Foundation, *Backgrounder*, "A Guide to Fixing Social Security, Medicare, and Medicaid," No. 2114, March 12, 2008.

69  The Heritage Foundation, *Backgrounder*, "A Guide to Fixing Social Security, Medicare, and Medicaid," No. 2114, March 12, 2008.

70  *The Wall Street Journal,* "Firms Face New Tax Curbs," May 4, 2009.

71  Tax Policy Center: 2010 Budget Tax Proposals, Tax Increases on High-Income Taxpayers, 2009.

72  The Heritage Foundation, *WebMemo,* "Economic Effects of Increasing the Tax Rates on Capital Gains and Dividends," No. 1891, April 15, 2008.

73  Taxing Democracy: Understanding Tax Avoidance and Evasion, edited by Valerie Braithwaite, Hampshire, England, Ashgate Publishing, 2003.

74  Taxing Democracy: Understanding Tax Avoidance and Evasion, edited by Valerie Braithwaite, Hampshire, England, Ashgate Publishing, 2003.

75  *Investment Advisor,* "Even Affluent Clients Feel the Chill," October 1, 2008.

# 7

# Under the Knife

As of this writing, a major national debate over healthcare and health insurance is taking place. The White House is pushing to essentially nationalize many healthcare functions. Proponents of nationalizing healthcare are insisting that the plans that passed the House and Senate, respectively, will lower costs across the board, while also covering more Americans, though not all Americans. America's healthcare debate is still evolving and no one can be sure of where the debate will lead.

Of the nation's proverbial $50 trillion mortgage referenced earlier in the book, healthcare obligations comprise some $32 trillion of it.[1] As it turns out, however, Americans don't see healthcare as just another of our country's economic challenges. I believe retirees see it as the mother of all economic challenges. Although healthcare made a cameo appearance in our national debate some 15 years ago, it has now come front and center, on the operating table, under the knife. Doctors have chimed in about it, and hospital associations have as well. Major American employers such as Wal-Mart have also been introduced into the conversation. Everyone has an opinion about American healthcare, but no one seems to have a really good diagnosis about what to do with it.

# How Did Healthcare Become Hellthcare?

No one can say for sure how we got to this point. What we do know is that we've developed a health system that is unparalleled anywhere in the world. The research and the pharmaceuticals developed as a result have served to extend and enhance the lives of Americans and all people who've been exposed to American healthcare. It hasn't always been that way. Only in the last century have we developed vaccinations and learned how to better control infectious diseases.[2] Infant mortality was relatively common just over a century ago, and now it's very rare, which has gone a long way toward extending the average lifespan of Americans and people the world over. Some cities and localities had health departments in the early 1900s, but it was the success of a county sanitation campaign to control a typhoid epidemic in Yakima County, Washington, in 1910–11 that helped drum up the desire for such agencies nationwide.[3] In 1955, Dr. Jonas Salk developed the polio vaccine, turning a scary, crippling disease into a memory not just here but also abroad. A story such as Dr. Salk's makes me very optimistic that cures and vaccines will be found for diseases that have become prevalent today. Back then, both the public sector and the private sector were making great strides in medicine that served to enhance the quality of life in America and, if my research is complete, finding any complaints about the costs was impossible.

It's equally difficult to find out exactly when the healthcare menagerie we have now came into existence. When did employer-provided health insurance become the norm? Did the need for insurance ever really intersect with market forces? And if they did intersect, did they simply collide and cause a big mess rather than bring together the buyer and seller of a service at a market-clearing price? That's the way it works in every other segment of our economy:

A product or service is offered at a price, and people decide whether that price is worthwhile for the product or service. But when it comes to healthcare, there's been a disruption in that consumer/producer relationship. Something has kept marketers from directly meeting the needs of the consumers who want or need the product. Whenever there is such a disruption between buyers and sellers of a product or service, resulting in a distortion of either the price or the quality of the product or service, you can be pretty sure that an outside agent has gotten involved—an outside agent whose job it is not to facilitate a solution, but rather to make itself important, a gatekeeper, a part of the process.

Presently, healthcare programs are largely offered by employers to their employees as part of a benefits package. In most cases, the employers pay part of each employee's health benefits, and the employee pays the rest. The money that the employer spends is subject to favorable tax treatment because the federal tax code excludes the value of employer-sponsored health insurance from the employee's income for the purposes of either income or payroll tax. The whole setup is a byproduct of wage and price controls imposed by the Roosevelt Administration during the World War II era. Today, this byproduct serves as a huge tax subsidy.[4] The result has been the wholesale distortion of price and product quality in an industry that's grown to represent approximately 20% of today's American economy.[5]

Some people lament that medicine as it's practiced today places too much emphasis on providers earning money and not enough on the business of helping people get better. In his 2002 book, *The Economic Evolution of American Health Care*, David Dranove draws upon the image of a loveable television character by writing that, due to all the bean counting, *"there seems to be little room for Marcus Welby in the modern health economy."* Quaint as the thought might be, doctors and hospitals and pharmaceutical companies and medical device manufacturers need to earn money if they're to pay their employees, continue to be a good investment for their stockholders, and stay in business long enough to be a part of the next generation of medical care. Although we never saw it on television, even Marcus Welby had to present a bill to his patients.

The real reason why healthcare is so expensive and is sometimes so difficult to attain has everything to do with the tax code. The fact is that the market for health products and services barely parallels the market for groceries or (to use the example of something more complicated) home computers. Unless you're a doctor or a computer engineer of some kind, you really can't have a good understanding of the intricacies of either medicine or computers. However, consumers of computers have navigated the computer market over the years because they've dealt directly with computer manufacturers or computer retailers. Computer makers have communicated with consumers in a way that consumers can understand, telling consumers what their products can do for them in a language they can understand, and consumers have made decisions based on that information. The result has been that the quality of computers has shot up considerably while prices have gone down. Consumers don't need to know all the jargon; they just need a product that will do what they want it to do. An even more modern-day example is flat-screen televisions. Just a few years ago they cost thousands of dollars. Today they're significantly less expensive, while their quality has improved. Why is that? It's not because consumers know anything more about terms like *1080P* and *scart sockets*; it's because retailers get to deal directly with consumers.

Consumers do not, however, deal directly with doctors in the traditional sense; very little about the present doctor/patient relationship resembles a free market. Sure, when they're going through a check-up of some kind, consumers are face-to-face with their doctors, but that's the extent of it. Before meeting with the doctor, a consumer has to find out if the doctor is part of her health plan. A change in one's employment situation could result in a need to switch doctors. This situation might cause many to not take a position that might otherwise be a great professional move. After the appointment, the patient makes a copayment of, say, $10 and then finds out in a couple weeks if the insurance company will pay the balance of the doctor visit. If not, the patient has to pay the balance for the doctor visit or put the remaining charge on a flex spending account, if that applies. In recent years, Medicare, the federal program to help the elderly, and Medicaid, the plan the states administer to help lower income citizens, have been reimbursing doctors less than the doctors have billed them. The result is that doctors have to bill their other patients more to make up the difference.

Some doctors are more aggressive in making up the difference. A small percentage of doctors have introduced the concept of Concierge Care into their practices. Concierge Care can be compared to the VIP passes that you would like to receive when going to a club, except you don't pay quite as much as you would for the VIP pass in a doctor's office. Patients pay an extra $1,500 to $2,500 yearly in conjunction with their insurance to receive this exclusive care.[6] A VIP patient can benefit from a shorter wait time, increased amount of visitation time with the doctor, 24/7 access to the doctor, and more extensive physical exams.[7] In 2008, only 1,000 U.S. doctors actually offered the VIP program, as the shift to personalized healthcare has been a gradual process while the debate of paying for extra medical attention continues.[8]

There's also the rapidly rising cost that doctors have to pay for their malpractice insurance premiums. In the absence of any kind of tort reform, doctors practice in constant fear of being sued for malpractice by lawyers who stand to receive multimillion dollar judgments. That leads to doctors ordering more and more tests and procedures for patients, just to defend themselves in case of a court appearance. Of course, those tests and procedures cost money and, just like escalating malpractice insurance, drive up the cost of healthcare. And let's face it; when doctors tell us that we need an MRI or a scan or a blood test because they're concerned, we listen. If they were operating in a sales world, doctors would go beyond what is called the "assumptive" close because they have actually mastered what should be called the "instructive" close, meaning they will tell us what to do and we will do it. Although second opinions may be common, we don't typically say, *"Let me get back to you on that test, doctor."*

Just for fun, let's compare health insurance to auto insurance. When my car was hit in an intersection a few years ago, I immediately turned to my insurance company to take care of the damage. As it turned out, the gentleman who hit me was uninsured, and my agent navigated through all the laws and paperwork associated with such a collision. In the meantime, he arranged for a loaner while my car was repaired, and the insurance company took care of all the bills. I don't know how much it cost to get my car back into working order, but that's the reason I pay the insurance premiums: to cover the need for big ticket repairs. The way we spend for auto insurance is different from the way we spend for healthcare. Let's use this spending hierarchy, created by American Economist Milton Friedman[9] to illustrate the difference. According to Friedman, people spend in four ways:

- Spending our own money on ourselves
- Spending our own money on other people
- Spending other people's money on ourselves
- Spending other people's money on other people

The first kind of spending results in the best value because the end user of a product or service is also the buyer—there's an optimum combination of budget control and quality control. The worst kind of spending is the fourth one because no one's performing any budget control, and no one's performing any quality control. Car insurance is operated along the lines of the first type of spending because you can compare insurance rates and coverages and make a decision that best suits you. When you make a claim, the insurance company is then spending its own money and makes decisions based on its best interests, one of which is keeping the customer satisfied enough to remain a customer. For relatively small things like oil changes or tires, you can make those decisions yourself about when you want to get them and how much you want to pay. Could you imagine having to clear a new set of spark plugs with your auto insurance company before you get them?

Healthcare insurance is operated along the lines of the fourth type of spending, with big employers (or groups of employers) getting together with insurance companies to decide what kind of coverage to offer to a vast and varied collection of employees. They're not beholden to the end users who pay their premiums as much as those end users are beholden to them; unlike in the car insurance business, the end users can't just pick up the phone and move their business to another insurance company if they're dissatisfied with the service.

After the employers make the decision about the plans they'll present to their employees, the employees are made to choose from among those plans—but first they need to see if their doctor is in a certain plan or if another plan might be better for a pre-existing condition or a current pregnancy. If all the stars don't align correctly, consumers must make concessions before they even see a doctor. Either the consumer has to change doctors or a child or spouse has to change doctors.

Purchasers of healthcare proclaim that because they can buy in large quantities for many employees, they're realizing extreme cost advantages. What these buyers are really doing is treating healthcare as a commodity, like oil or copper. It's as if healthcare did the same thing for everyone. To exacerbate the problem, employers receive favorable tax treatment for the portion of the employee healthcare premiums they pay, so employees have very little appreciation of how much is spent on their behalf for their healthcare. The result is that the end users—the employees—are not allowed to do the actual shopping and comparing of similar plans offered by health insurance companies (which would go a long way toward proper and accurate price discovery). They have limited budget control and limited quality control; the result is that healthcare is more expensive than it needs to be and less effective than it can be.

The same can be said about Medicare and Medicaid. For the purposes of our retirement discussion, I'll concentrate on Medicare. In 1965, LBJ signed the Medicare bill as part of his Great Society platform. When the program was enacted the following year, Medicare's annual cost was $3 billion.[10] Nearly 30 years later, a House Ways and Means Committee estimate pinned the cost at $12 billion in 1990.[11] This supposedly conservative estimate was off by just a few dollars, because actual Medicare expenditures that year turned out to be $107 billion.[12] Of course, the program's cost has shot up since then to $2 trillion in 2006 and is only expected to continue rising into the stratosphere.[13]

# Settling for the Best

As measured by its mere quality, our healthcare continues to be the best in the world. We continue to research and invent pharmaceuticals and procedures that past generations may have never dreamed possible. We have routinely extended life expectancy to the point where many retirees are now living healthy, active lives. They're running, they're riding bicycles, they're skiing, and they're traveling the world. Former president George H.W. Bush even celebrated his 85th birthday on June 12, 2009, by taking a parachute jump, just as he did to celebrate his 75th and 80th birthdays. But while celebrating all that we can do during a healthy retirement, we've been neglecting its cost and the multiplier effect of higher healthcare costs combined with a population that is living longer than ever.

The first thing you need to do about your long-term healthcare is convince yourself that the government may not help you with it. Sure Medicare may still be around a decade or two from now, but chances are that it won't look anything like it does now. And the unfunded liability that Medicaid piles into the states will no doubt trigger a change in the way that program is administered in the future. Before you say that's a good thing, allow me to say that whatever Medicare looks like a decade or two from now will likely be worse. It will probably have some sort of means testing; it will probably take more out of everyone's paycheck or retirement income; it will probably be even more inefficient than it is now. Therefore, you must forget that there is any government healthcare program and make healthcare during your retirement your own responsibility. And how do you do that? You treat healthcare as the financial obligation it is and start planning ahead. In the next ten years, 50 million Americans will be 65 or older and more than half of them will require at least one year of long-term care, whereas 20% will need more than five years of such care.[14] By 2030 one in every five Americans will be 65 or older.[15] That will require long-term care insurance that will fully cover the year of care. How much will that cost? Well, in 2008 that total was $85,000—and it can only go up from there.[16]

Medical care continues to take up a larger and larger chunk of the American retiree's budget. A recent Consumer Price Index Summary report shows that medical care went up 3.4% from 2008 to 2009.[17]

That's during a decade when we had virtually no inflation! *"There is no way a laborer can pay for any serious healthcare in this nation,"* said a 49-year-old woman we talked to in our focus group who works in a blue collar job and has been uninsured for years. If these numbers are alarming to you, that's probably a good thing because it shows you that the best healthcare in the world costs money. These numbers also show you what incomplete planning can do to your retirement nest egg and why somewhere between 70% to 75% of all long-term care given in the United States is provided by a family member.[18]

# Look to the Past, Look Abroad, and Look into the Future

Some may say that the rising cost of healthcare is simply a positive reflection of the ever-improving healthcare coverage we have in this country. Others simply call it a problem and turn to the government for a solution. The second group is carrying the day right now. Similar national conversations predated the signing of the original Medicare bill in 1965 and all other addendums, leading up to the Prescription Drug Act signed by the 43rd President of the United States. The more government control of healthcare, the more rationing there is. A simple look across our northern border can reveal that fact, as costs keep going up and the quality of service keeps going down. A wry joke used by many opposed to a government takeover of healthcare in this country is, *"Where will the Canadians go to get quality healthcare?"* Only those Canadians who have enough disposable income to come to the United States can get vital, and even lifesaving, procedures done in a timely fashion. If they stay home, they need to wait in line.

A government-run healthcare system in the United States could make this entire chapter moot, but that doesn't mean it would improve your chances of building up a retirement nest egg. Just the opposite: Such a system may be so unwieldy and expensive that taxes would skyrocket, and you'd have a hard time finding enough discretionary income to put away for retirement. According to the Tax Foundation, under a new plan, couples making more than $1 million a year will be taxed an additional 5.4% surtax, pushing a top tax rate to 39.6%.[19] As things stand now, however, you can't wait to learn how a new healthcare plan might unfold in your retirement. You can't wait to financially plan for healthcare in retirement. It doesn't matter how good you feel now or how many years away you are from the end of your working life; statistics and trends reveal that there's an extremely good chance that you're going to need more medical care as you get older. You're going to need assistance to do some of the things you do now. Your health could also become a bone of contention among family members if you do not plan ahead. Your children and siblings could very well argue about who needs to take care of you, how best to take care of you, and what to do when there's not enough money to take care of you.

### Pre-Meltdown, Healthcare on Shaky Ground

For years before the Meltdown of 2008, retirement in America was already threatened by rising costs and rising anxiety. Even though more and more people began living longer and enjoying active retirements, statistics showed that healthcare and the reliance on government for it was threatening the whole concept of retirement.

- Unexpected medical bills have been the main reason that Americans 65 and older were the fastest growing group seeking bankruptcy protection.[20]
- Estimates anticipate an average 65-year-old couple will spend more than $300,000 out of pocket to cover healthcare costs that aren't covered by Medicare.[21]
- Medicare was predicted to run out of money in 2019, Social Security in 2041—but is now expected to be exhausted four years sooner, in 2037.[22] If Social Security's demise was so accelerated pre-meltdown, how quickly will Medicare tap out?
- Forty-six million Americans were reportedly without health insurance.[23]
- The cost of brand name drugs has increased more than 2.5 times the rate of general inflation since 2002.[24]
- Starting in the 1990s, seniors' debt levels began surging as their incomes failed to keep up with housing, energy, and especially, healthcare costs.[25]

### Post-Meltdown, on Shaky Ground During an Earthquake

The economic meltdown that took place in the fall of 2008 hit everyone hard. As people's reduced personal worth came to the forefront, it was difficult to prioritize which issue needed to be addressed first. But one problem seemed to grow a little bit faster than any other.

- The Medicare forecasts changed; it's now expected to run out of money in 2017 and Social Security in 2037.[26]
- One-fourth of Medicare beneficiaries can expect to see sharply higher premiums, from $96.40 per month today to $120 per month in 2011.[27]
- Since December 2007, the American economy has shed 7.1 million jobs,[28] which has increased pressure on Medicaid, as every single percentage point rise in the unemployment rate means approximately 1 million people turn to Medicaid. (Another 1.1 million go uninsured.)[29]

In the coming year, Medicare spending is expected to increase faster than either workers' earnings or the economy overall.[30] If cost controls are not successful in producing the expected savings, Congress will no doubt turn to tax increases to preserve benefits. The possibility of taxing the medical benefits of employed workers has been floated on more than one occasion during the 111th Congress and is likely to be brought up again. The effect will be that workers who have gotten used to and budgeted for their current income level might now have to pay taxes on additional income in the form of healthcare benefits—income they never physically see. If such a tax plan goes through, the effect will be devastating on discretionary income, discretionary spending, and the overall health of the economy. Understanding behaviors that may be obstacles to incorporating healthcare into your retirement planning is a first step toward making sure that healthcare doesn't become *hellthcare*.

# The Retirement Brain Game

**Illusion of knowledge**—Having an assumption or belief and assuming that any information learned at a later date will simply bolster that assumption or belief when, in fact, much of that information can contradict the earlier-held belief—for example, assuming Medicare will cover something but not knowing all the facts.

**Overconfidence**—A bias that dictates a person entering into a new venture does not know how he will do at it. If he has early success, he will attribute that success to his ability instead of to other circumstances that may not be in his control; people enter retirement in great health, for instance, and become overconfident about maintaining that health.

**Anchoring**—Tying a current belief to a past one, like estimating the level of health and health costs based on preretirement age and not adjusting to the potential of health diminishing with age. Perceptual spending biases that cause many of us to overspend on brands can also affect our healthcare spending. For example, an experiment conducted by Dan Ariely, a behavioral economist at Duke University, showed that people believe more expensive drugs are more effective. People said they felt better taking a pill that cost $2.50 than one that cost 10 cents, even though both pills were Vitamin C.[31]

### Know, You Don't

Regarding no other retirement subject is the *illusion of knowledge* more evident than when the subject is healthcare. The problem is, healthcare is a constantly changing subject, both for citizens and for industry practitioners. Just think about kids in the early 1950s before Dr. Salk discovered the polio vaccine: They and their parents had to live in nearly constant fear of this disabling disease. They knew that one day a kid could be fine, and a week later he could be sick in bed, never again able to use his legs. Dr. Salk's discovery not only solved a terrible problem with the population, but it also allowed medical researchers to spend their efforts on other illnesses. Basically, one discovery changed the whole face of healthcare. Because so many peripheral things, such as medical research, affect healthcare, government affairs, finance, and the overall economy, you can never know everything you need to know about the subject. So many new pieces of information seem to contradict earlier information that living a healthy life is like hitting a moving target. Remember when bran was suddenly heralded as the newest health food hero? As quickly as people ran out to fill up their cupboards with the latest varieties of trendy bran cereals, the news came revealing that even bran in excessive amounts has a few drawbacks.

Doctors and researchers are learning more about the human body every day: what makes it tick, what makes it better, what makes it a mystery so that—even after collective centuries of constant study—it is still full of more questions than answers. Doctors do not suffer from the *illusion of knowledge* because the very nature of their profession is to learn more and more every day. The only thing you know about your health is how you feel right now. You have a general understanding of why you feel that way and what to do and avoid doing if you want to maintain your health. Your doctor can certainly help guide you in the right direction as your body gets older, but you'll never have all the answers about keeping yourself healthy. The only thing you can do right now is appreciate what got you here, do what you think is right to keep you healthy in the future, and make sure you have a plan in place that will allow you to have enough money to pay the people who are going to take care of you when you can't.

### From Pizza to Pepto

If you live long enough, you'll get sick no matter how healthy you are. Actually, you've probably been sick before: a cold, a flu, or food poisoning. It's not fun and it's frustrating to take time to recover, but after a week or two you feel back to normal—like nothing happened. So the next time you get sick, you'll probably feel pretty confident about your eventual recovery. That confidence may just be **overconfidence**. Being overconfident about the future state of your health is a behavioral finance bias that can prevent you from adequately planning for the amount of money you will need should you become disabled or require long-term care.

These days, many people are entering retirement with *overconfidence* about their health. They're active, they're traveling, they're eating the foods they've always enjoyed, that have always helped keep them healthy, and all that is terrific. However, just because these people have entered retirement in such great shape doesn't mean they're going to stay in great shape as they age. In the future, they'll need drugs and treatment they don't need today. If you've had years of great health, congratulations are in order. But don't get overconfident about your health in the future. Plan while you're still healthy to make sure that you'll get the kind of treatment many people like you eventually need. Setting up long-term care while you're still healthy can go a long way toward protecting your grown children from emotional decisions and expenses that could hit them hard if they are seriously underprepared. A story I read recently detailed that some retirees have stopped questioning their physicians and pharmacists about side effects and dosing for their medicine; now their questioning is entirely about cost! In fact, some people who are too well-off for government health insurance, but can't afford their own insurance, are often weighing the needs of taking maintenance medications against more immediate needs, like food and shelter.[32]

When you retire, you will likely be on a fixed income. It may be a large income or it may be a small one, but you can rest assured that your health will require more attention and more money during your retirement. Indeed, your health will take a bigger percentage of your budget every day, every month, every year. People in and approaching retirement in most of the past decade have *"debt loads that their parents would not have considered,"* according to Sally Hurme of the AARP.[33] Don't be overconfident about your health or the certainty of government programs to be there for you. Don't procrastinate: Start planning *now* for your medical future because your medical needs will meet you there.

Some of the people we spoke to at our focus groups had some interesting assumptions and hopes for their retirement when it came to healthcare. We found multiple examples of what could be called *CATCH 62*, those eligible to collect Social Security at age 62, but even if retired, are not eligible for Medicare until age 65. One of our focus group participants was forced to retire at 62 from her bookkeeping job and had to sell her house to pay for escalating healthcare and prescription drug costs. We also met two uninsured women, both 62 years old, who perhaps exhibited *overconfidence* in their own health and in the government. The first woman said, *"My mother lived to be 83 and never saw a doctor. All I have to do is go two more years from this July, and I will be entitled to whatever medical care goes to seniors."* The other woman said that she and her husband *"are anxiously watching the President's attempts at restructuring healthcare."*

### *Anchors Weigh*

People tend to **anchor** themselves to what they know and how they feel when it comes to their healthcare. For example, if you saw the doctor once each of the previous ten years for a checkup, then you may be fairly confident that you'll see the doctor only once again this year. But that's not necessarily the case. Our bodies are constantly changing, and many of those changes require us to see the doctor a little more often as time goes on. A person can go through his 20s and never need to see a doctor. But that same person in his 40s will need annual checkups and will likely have to make a few adjustments. His eyes may require correctional lenses, for instance. His everyday jog may need to turn into a bike ride to lessen the impact on his knees. Big or sudden physical changes naturally lead to *adjustment*, but when everything appears to stay the same, people don't think about adjusting. The changes in our bodies can be so gradual, we think one year is like another is like another. But the truth is that we get older every day, and it's important to be aware that the day will come when more attention is paid to your health. More doctor visits. More medicine. More restrictions on diet. More healthcare costs in retirement.

As *Grumpy Old Man* Walter Matthau said, *"My doctor gave me six months to live, but when I couldn't pay the bill, he gave me six months more."* It's impossible to say what healthcare costs will be in the next year or the next ten years. But we can be reasonably sure that they will be higher than they are today. It will cost more in the way of taxes, it will cost more of your discretionary income, and it will take up a bigger percentage of your overall income before and in retirement.

## Transparent Versus Opaque

Your nest egg can be put into a savings account or invested in a way of your choosing. Health insurance is harder to see and is sometimes a little tougher to spend money on because you really don't want to use your insurance for anything more than an occasional check-up. But don't give in to the desire to eliminate your insurance altogether just to pay off bills or build up a nest egg: If you're uninsured for a catastrophic event, the medical bills will diminish your money or even bankrupt you. When you need the benefits of health insurance, healthcare coverage becomes completely transparent.

| Transparent | Opaque | Takeaway |
|---|---|---|
| A nest egg is built with the vision and perception of a happy, healthy retirement in mind. | A healthcare plan during retirement is based on uncertainty and the illusion that government and family will prevail when necessary. | Estimates anticipate an average 65-year-old couple may need $300,000 out-of-pocket to cover healthcare costs that aren't covered by Medicare in retirement, and 30% of America's Medicare budget is spent on participants' last years of life.[34] Healthcare must be accounted for in your retirement nest egg. |

# Improve Your Retirementology IQ

When it comes to retirement healthcare, it's important to keep in mind that you're going to need the same thing for it that you'll need for most other aspects of your retirement: You're going to need money. The more, the better. There's no telling exactly how much you'll need, but that's the case with retirement income as well. The important thing is that you overcome the simple human emotion to *procrastinate* and start preparing as early as possible for your retirement healthcare. But remember, healthcare takes more than money. It takes knowing what to do with the money to get the best healthcare you can possibly get for your retirement.

### Take Advantage of Mental Budgeting to Account for Healthcare Expenditures

You probably have an idea of when you'll retire. But you never know when you'll need more in the way of healthcare. Chances are that when you're young, you won't have much of a need for health-care—a great percentage of the people in this country who are presently uninsured are people in their 20s who've decided not to pay for health insurance. If you're in that group, you have more discretionary income than you would otherwise have. It's a perfect opportunity for you to put that money into an account that you can use specifically for healthcare when you get older.

### *Determine What Benefits Your Coverage Will Provide When You Reach 65 Years Old*

Under the banner of planning ahead, you need to look into what you may need when you reach 65. Check with your parents, as they may provide you with the closest thing that you can get to a roadmap regarding what's ahead for you. Compare what you learn to what your present coverage provides, and then start looking into ways to patch the leaks ahead of time. Remember, overcoming *procrastination* now and determining what you'll need in the future could save you an awful lot of money that you can use for other aspects of your retirement.

### *Determine if You Can Take Your Present Coverage into Retirement*

Don't just assume that you can take your present insurance into retirement with you. And don't just listen to what you want to hear about trying to do so. That would be suffering greatly from the *illusion of knowledge*. You may be happy with your present coverage and what it costs you, and you may be able to take it into retirement with you. If so, that's great because you can avoid changing doctors, changing providers, and all the hassle and paperwork involved in such a move. But make sure you don't go into retirement with your present carrier just because you want to avoid all that claptrap. And don't *anchor* yourself to what you're paying now or the service you're receiving now. Retirement will be a time when your needs will change—you'll have to adjust with them.

## Consider Buying Disability Insurance to Ensure Retirement Income

Disability is known as *"the forgotten risk."*[35] But you should know that, at any given age, the chances of becoming disabled are higher than the chances of dying. One in seven workers suffers a five-year or longer period of disability before they're 65,[36] so don't get *overconfident* about your ability to earn a living. Fewer and fewer employers are offering disability insurance than life insurance, and it's actually much tougher to qualify for disability—just refer to the previous statistic. You may want to consider disability insurance as early in life as possible.

## Keep Records of All Medical Expenses and Reimbursements

Having a paper trail can help you make a *mental accounting* of the things you may need in the future. If your use of a certain drug or treatment is trending upward, then you may need to account for that in the years to come and set aside a little more. If your present employer has a flex spending plan, you may be able to pay for minor medical needs, such as glasses, with pretax money. Remember, healthcare is expensive, and it's only going to get more so, so take advantage of every loophole the law allows.

As things evolve, there's no telling where they will end. Will we have an entirely government-run system? Will that leave us with any healthcare options? Will we decide to go to Canada when the wait here for an operation is too long? Will the members of Congress who lobby for the "public option" think enough of the plan to give up their own gold-plated healthcare program? And after all the taxing is done to pay for the system, will there be any money left in anyone's pocket? Or will things get better as they pertain to a more market-oriented system of healthcare? If so, will pricing pressures keep costs in check and quality on the rise? Or will the politicians just kick the can down the road for the next Congress and the next administration?

## Don't Spread Yourself Too Thick

Hard as it may be to believe, it is possible to be overinsured; to buy coverages that overlap when one policy would cover what you need. People who travel and rent a car often opt for the insurance coverage offered with the rental car, which is exactly like the coverage they have for their own car. A simple call to their car insurance agent can tell them if they need any extra coverage for a rental, but few make that call. Instead, they overinsure themselves when they're out of town and pay a lot to do it with money that could be spent more wisely. The same can happen with healthcare insurance. A couple may buy insurance at their separate employers when a plan at one employer can cover both of them more efficiently. It's human nature to be overly cautious, especially when the economy is hitting a rough patch, but you have to overcome that natural tendency when it comes to something as important as health insurance. You may want to consider long-term care insurance, as well as disability insurance, in the case of job loss. Tell your loved ones—the people who depend on you—what your plans are for your retirement healthcare and your long-term care. Remember, they've counted on you all their lives: Turning the tables on them and becoming one of their dependents is a difficulty you don't want in a familial relationship. The sooner you get going on this all-important planning, the better off everyone will be.

**HEALTHCARE POLICY AND EXPENSE HAVE THE POTENTIAL TO SABOTAGE YOUR RETIREMENT PLAN.**

# Endnotes

1 The Pew Charitable Trusts, Financial Report: Entitlement Programs Underfunded by Trillions, December 16, 2008.

2 Centers for Disease Control and Prevention, *MMWR Weekly*, "Ten Great Public Health Achievements—United States, 1900–1999," December 24, 1999.

3 Centers for Disease Control and Prevention, *MMWR Weekly*, "Achievements in Public Health, 1900-1999: Changes in the Public Health System," December 24, 1999.

4   The Heritage Foundation, *WebMemo*, "Health Care Reform: Changing the Tax Treatment of Health Insurance," No. 2344, March 16, 2009.

5   *Healthcare Finance News*, "Economist says healthcare reform bill will raise spending to 20 percent GDP 'much before 2017,'" August 6, 2009.

6   *Physician's News Digest*, "Hybrid model for concierge medicine," December 2007.

7   *Physician's News Digest*, "Hybrid model for concierge medicine," December 2007.

8   *Time*, "Giving Patients the VIP Treatment," May 14, 2008.

9   The Total Package, "Milton Friedman Explains It All...," 2009.

10  *Reason Magazine*, "The Medicare Monster," January 1993.

11  *Reason Magazine*, "The Medicare Monster," January 1993.

12  *Reason Magazine*, "The Medicare Monster," January 1993.

13  *The New York Times*, "Health Spending Exceeded Record $2 Trillion in 2006," January 8, 2008.

14  U.S. Department of Health and Human Services, National Clearinghouse for Long-Term Care Information, "What is Long-Term Care," October 22, 2008.

15  University of Nebraska Medical Center, *UNMC Today*, "UNMC breaks ground on the new Home Instead of Center for Successful Aging," September 24, 2008.

16  SFGate, "Save $85,000 for long-term care Fidelity says," June 26, 2008.

17  U.S. Bureau of Labor Statistics, Consumer Price Index Summary—December 2009, January 15, 2010.

18  Long Term Care Link.net, "About Long Term Care at Home," 2009.

19  Tax Foundation, *Fiscal Fact*, "New House Health Care Plan: Income Surtax is Modified in $1.05 Trillion Bill," No. 200, October 30, 2009.

20  *USA Today*, "Retirees up against debt," January 22, 2007.

21  Yahoo! Finance, "The Health Scare Lurking in Your Retirement Plan," September 5, 2008.

22  *The New York Times*, "Recession Drains Social Security and Medicare," May 13, 2009.

23  *New York Daily News*, "Census Bureau: Number of Americans without health insurance rises to 46.3 million," September 10, 2009.

24  *USA Today*, "Brand-name drug prices continue to grow," March 4, 2008.

25  *USA Today*, "Retirees up against debt," January 22, 2007.

26  *The Washington Post*, "Alarm Sounded On Social Security," May 13, 2009.

27  *The New York Times*, "Recession Drains Social Security and Medicare," May 13, 2009.

28  Market Watch, "Job losses expected to slow to 167,000 in September," October 1, 2009.

29  Kaiser Commission on Medicaid and the Uninsured, "Turning to Medicaid and SCHIP in an Economic Recession: Conversations with Recent Applications and Enrollees," December 2008.

30  *The New York Times*, "Recession Drains Social Security and Medicare," May 13, 2009.

31  Workforce Management, "People-Proof Your Health Benefits," May 2009.

32  *The New York Times*, "Slump Pushing Cost of Drugs Out of Reach," June 4, 2009.

33  *USA Today*, "Retirees up against debt," March 2, 2007.

34  Yahoo! Finance, "The Health Scare Lurking in Your Retirement Plan," September 5, 2008; *American Medical News*, "End-of-life care provision stirs angst in health reform debate," August 24, 2009.

35  MSN Money, "Disability insurance can save your life," August 20, 2008.

36  MSN Money, "Disability insurance can save your life," August 20, 2008.

take many shapes. It may be as basic as simple math—adding, subtracting, or applying simple interest. Or it can be much more convoluted. But complexity in the financial world can also be represented by sheer size. The size of a financial problem can become so big that our ability to comprehend it is compromised. We shrug our shoulders, shake our heads, and insist that the subject be changed to something a bit easier to understand, like molecular microbiology, for example.

The numbers that are represented by the deficit our federal government has nurtured over the years are the perfect example of complexity via size. Many people are confused by the numbers thrown around. We have heard numbers such as $1.4 trillion, $12 trillion, and $383 billion. Many of these are used to describe both debt and deficit. The deficit is the difference between what the government takes in, called receipts, and outlays, which is what the government spends, which includes Social Security and Medicare benefits. When there is a deficit, the Treasury must borrow money needed for the government to pay the bills. The government's accumulated deficits are essentially the government's debt. The Congressional Budget Office estimated our deficit for 2009 was $1.4 trillion (about 10% of the Gross Domestic Product), but that is not the extent of our "debt."[2] Not by a long shot. According to an article in *The Wall Street Journal*, as of September 30, 2009, the national debt was almost $12 trillion, and interest on that debt was $383 billion for the year, according to the Treasury Department's Bureau of the Public Debt. In August 2009, the White House Office of Management and Budget (OMB) estimated total government revenues at about $2 trillion. The revenue estimate included $904 billion from individual income taxes. This means the cost of interest on the debt represented more than 40 cents of every dollar that came in from individual income taxes.[3] It's gotten to the point where I recently saw a bumper sticker that read, *"Don't tell Washington what comes after trillion."* Then I saw another one that read, *"Are you better off than you were $4 trillion ago?"* The numbers are tossed around in such a cavalier fashion that many people stop discerning between a million, a billion, and a trillion. But the difference is astonishing.

Consider this example: Imagine that I offer to buy you and your significant other a nice weekend in Vegas. How much would you need for a fun-filled weekend there? Would $10,000 do the trick? When I ask that of most people, they indicate that it would. That's probably enough for first-class airfare, a very nice hotel, a nice dinner, a limo, and even some fun at the tables. Well, if I gave you that $10K in $100 bills, the stack of those bills would be about 1/2" high—not exactly, but a close enough proxy. What if I told you that I would make the same offer to 99 of your best friends? How tall would the $1M stack of $100 bills be to support this generous gift? It would be somewhere around 5 feet tall.

But we are still not tackling the kinds of dollars that are spent today. No; today, our nation's vocabulary has the word "trillion" popping up a lot more frequently. How high would that pile of money be if it contained $1 trillion of $100 bills? Common responses to that question might be, *"30 feet!"* or *"The height of the Empire State Building!"* or *"As high as the length of three football fields!"* Not even close. Would you believe 789 miles tall? That's about the height of 144 Mt. Everests! That's a lot of *"Benjamins,"* as the kids say. Or look at it this way: If a bunch of free-spending senators laid that trillion-dollar stack down in Washington and started driving west, they'd get to Fort Wayne, Indiana, before they came to the end of the $100 bills. If all these lengths, numbers, and distances sound overly complex to you, it's probably because you've reached the point where you are numbed by numbers. *Number numbness* is the tendency for a person to be simply overwhelmed by large numbers, such as government cost estimates and projections, or by all the baggage associated with the allusive "number" representing a retiree's nest egg. And this numbness often leads to apathy and inertia. I have had some advisers tell me that they avoid the conversation of "the magic number" with some clients because, if they hear the actual amount, their eyes roll back in their heads and they give up altogether. The thinking seems to be that it is better to get them moving toward the goal to some degree. For some clients, this is probably true.

Just like a single dollar is pretty easy to understand, so is a single second in time. It's so quick that it passes fleetingly. Blink your eyes and a second is gone. Blink your eyes 86,400 times in a row and a whole day is gone. So given that knowledge, you might think that a million seconds could go by pretty quickly, and you'd be right. You probably remember what you were doing a million seconds ago because it happened just 13 days in the past. You likely remember where you were, whom you were with, and what you were doing. Your memory of a billion seconds in the past, though, may get a bit foggy. That's because a billion seconds ago it was the late 1970s and the Bee Gees' *Saturday Night Fever* album was topping the charts.[4] You may not remember where you were then or who you were with, but you can be pretty sure that your hair was feathered and whatever you were wearing would embarrass you today. By the way, one trillion seconds ago western civilization didn't yet exist. In fact, *civilized* society didn't exist, as Neanderthals roamed the plains of Europe.

A single second, like a single dollar, is small. But when money and time is piled up, it can add up amazingly. That's a lesson for anyone who's at all intimidated by the numbers involved in adding up the money needed for retirement. Think of it this way: Every large amount starts as a small amount. Although it may sound too simple, the key to turning that small amount into a larger amount is time and discipline. Understanding the importance of time and discipline is a major component to understanding Retirementology.

## The Retirement Brain Game

**Number numbness**—The tendency for a person to be simply overwhelmed by numbers presented, mainly because the numbers are so big that the person can't comprehend exactly how big they are.

**Bigness bias**—Whether it's inflation or compound interest, people have a tendency to overlook small numbers such as 1% or 2%. However, over time, those numbers become big. So whether people are paying a small percentage per year on their credit card interest or earning small interest on an account, the overall sum that is paid or earned is actually very big.

**Hindsight bias**—People often believe, after the fact, that some event was predictable and obvious when it was not predictable based on the information they had before the event took place. A person who's unsure about making an investment might believe, after the investment goes up, that he did have the information ahead of time that told him that the investment would be a positive one.

### Number Numbness Multiplied by Three

In their book *Why Smart People Make Big Money Mistakes and How to Correct Them,* authors Gary Belsky and Thomas Gilovich report the three ways that **number numbness** can affect long-term financial plans. The first is that you don't take taxes and inflation into effect. The second is that failure to understand the odds and the role of chance can cause you to make unwise financial decisions. Third, many people have an indifference to small numbers, and that bias can cost them big bucks when it comes to their financial plans over time.

*Failing to account for taxes and inflation.* Let's take a look at inflation. Many of you remember the inflation of the late '70s and early '80s. It was well into double digits and spawned something called the Misery Index, which combined the unemployment rate at the time with the inflation rate. The result of all this was an economic "malaise" that no one wants to repeat. Measuring inflation then was easy. Anybody who had a loan or wanted to borrow money was reminded of it daily. In December 1978, the prime rate (defined as the base rate on corporate loans posted by at least 75% of the nation's 30 largest banks) stood at a now unfathomable 11.75%.[5] Yet within 2 years, by December 1980, the prime rate had skyrocketed even further to a record 21.5%.[6] Increased borrowing costs squeezed the budgets of corporations and individuals, and economic activity was essentially choked off. Rates can also exemplify the problem of failing to account for inflation.

Since 1982, America has embarked on a tremendous economic expansion that would take us through the dot.com bust at the millennium. During that period there was only one recession of note. But one thing that people forget about during that era of general prosperity is that inflation still existed. It may have been 1% or 2% annually, but it was still there. Even at that low level, inflation was doing what it always does: taking away purchasing power from consumers, especially consumers on a fixed income, such as retirees. Because the rate

of inflation was relatively low, however, people didn't pay much attention to it. Instead, they looked at their nominal returns over those
years. A person who invested in the stock market on January 29, 1982,
when the DJIA was 871.10, didn't necessarily have 12.5 times more
buying power with that money on January 31, 2000, when the Dow
was 10,940.53.[7] Many dollars that were invested in the stock market
in 1982 and stayed there for the following 18 years increased many
times in value, at a rate that far outpaced inflation. With the benefit of
hindsight, this period looks like the Golden Age of stock investing, a
time when investors felt they could wade into the market with great
confidence that their principal would return a healthy profit. Today,
that mindset seems like a quaint memory of a bygone era exacerbated
by a press that seems all too willing to predict the next recession.

   *The role of odds and chance.* Although there is much skill, reason,
and understanding involved in making a good investment, these findings reflect how *number numbness* keeps investors from understanding the odds and role of chance in their investing. There's nothing any
single investor can do about the facts presented here, and it's not
dumb luck that has produced these kinds of returns over time. But
the numbers can be intimidating, and a short-term loss can scare an
investor away. Such findings as these make a pretty good case for the
buy-and-hold strategy of investing, but the stock market is only one
part of a retirement planning strategy you could consider. There are
any number of other ways you can accumulate a nest egg—all those
ways simply have to fall within your risk tolerance and comfort zone.

   Such a stance can keep you from succumbing to a mind trick
called **hindsight bias**. *"People who experience hindsight bias misap-
ply current hindsight to past foresight,"* according to Hersh Shefrin in
his book *Beyond Greed and Fear*. The previously held emotion may
not have been terribly strong, but the subsequent experience can
reinforce the emotion to the point where you think your premonition
was just as strong. If you were making an investment in a commodity
such as grain, and a grain investment that year turned out to be lousy
because of weather, you may say after the fact that you should have
known the weather would not be good for your investment. But no
one can predict the weather for an entire growing season, especially
when a single storm could negate an otherwise optimal growing season. We had a tremendous snowstorm here in Colorado a couple

years ago that swept through in a hurry and delivered several feet of snow. The storm came in so quickly that many ranchers could not get out to their fields to retrieve their cattle and get them under shelter, which resulted in huge financial losses for the ranchers. Odds and chance also play a part in long-term investing.

Finally, there's the part of *number numbness* called **bigness bias**. Think about the reference to inflation I covered a few paragraphs ago. During the late '70s, inflation was easy to notice because it was in the double digits. From 1982–2000, it was almost impossible to notice because it was often at only 1% or 2% annually. Because investors simply saw the big stock returns during this 18-year-long bull market, they didn't realize that inflation was actually taking a little bit of the purchasing power out of the dollars they were earning.[8] To look at it another way, when something is incrementally small, such as 1% inflation or a 2% annual return on an investment, you tend to overlook it, as it falls into that opaque category we have discussed throughout the book. But small numbers add up to big numbers. For example, hypothetically, if you pay 4% for a loan when you could pay 3%, that 1% can add up to a big number and can make a big difference in one's retirement plans over time.

# Investor Errors of Miscalculation

Numbers are the essence of evaluating outcomes and opportunities in investing, involving time, rate of return, and magnitude of losses and gains. Unfortunately, when you involve more than a couple of variables, people often become confused and make the wrong decision. Our tendency to miscalculate can impact everyday decisions. Are you a basketball fan?

### Down by Two, Seconds Remaining, What Play Do You Call?

Let's say, for example, that in basketball, the odds of making any given two-point shot are about one in two, or 50%. The odds of making any given three-point shot are about one in three, or 33%. So, if you have the ball and just a few ticks left on the clock and your team is down by two points, what play do you call for your team? The vast majority of coaches call for a two-point play in hopes of tying the game and sending it into overtime. The odds of them winning with such a strategy are about one in four, or 25%. This is because victory is dependent upon two consecutive events: making the shot and then winning in overtime, both with 50/50 chances of happening.

### Option A—Go for the Win

Shoot the three-point shot

Odds of making: 33%

### Option B—Play for Overtime

Shoot the two-point shot

Odds of making: 50%

Win the game in overtime

Odds of winning: 50%

25% chance of tying game AND going on to win in overtime

Pure number crunchers would say the hands-down better play is to shoot the three because it provides an 8% higher chance of victory. Some basketball traditionalists, on the other hand, might argue that you try to extend the game by taking the easier two-point shot and then try to win in overtime. A coach is rarely criticized for following "prevailing wisdom" by going for the tie and overtime. But is it the right call?

It might be tempting to summarize this issue and conclude that the technical analysis tells you to take the three-point shot. Using this logic, one colleague of mine—a well-published behavioral economist—argued vehemently with me that this was the best course of action. However, he never played basketball and seemed to be missing an understanding that "averages" can delude very easily, and some other complex factors are involved in this scenario. For example

- Does your team have, or lack, exceptionally good three-point shooters (as compared to the average)?
- Is the other team particularly good (or poor) at defending the three-point shot?
- Are you playing in front of the home crowd or on the road?
- What's the timeout situation?

When you consider all the factors that must be processed, interpreted, and used to make a split-second decision, it becomes clear why the guy two rows from the top of the arena does not get a vote in which play is called. It is precisely this complexity, and a coach's ability to sort through the noise and make the decision that gives his team the win, that determines his success or failure, and ultimately his career.

When it comes to our financial playbook, the situation is eerily similar. We receive many inputs from number crunchers and behavioral experts alike. At the highest levels, we may understand the rules of thumb when it comes to how much we need to plan for retirement, and perhaps even how our personal biases tend to discourage the behaviors necessary for success. However, that understanding alone is overly simplistic and disregards a host of complex and intertwined variables. For example

- How much can you afford to take from your portfolio each year in retirement?
- Will you need to make adjustments to the income you take to account for inflation?
- How will changes in tax rates impact your retirement plans and what can you do to insulate yourself from uncertainty?
- How can you resist temptation to chase market performance and hide from market rallies?
- What options are available to capitalize on your beliefs of where the economy, markets, and tax rates are headed?

Fortunately, like the team owner who employs a highly qualified coach, you have the opportunity to work with a highly qualified adviser who can process the variety of inputs and help keep you on the right path to your financial goals. Let's consider another example: taxi drivers.

A lot of taxi drivers make a serious monetary miscalculation when they quit working after attaining a given daily goal. For example, they might go home after they have earned $200. Predetermining the amount of money they intend to earn in a day is a benchmarking mistake, as each day presents different variables that can make it a good day or a bad day for a cab driver. The result is that they end up working much shorter hours on the very lucrative rainy days, when everyone is looking for a cab, and giving up the opportunity to earn much more money. Conversely, when a cabbie works much longer hours on sunny days when cabs are plentiful, he gives up the opportunity to do something that may be more profitable or enjoyable than trying to meet the $200 threshold he's set for himself driving the cab. "*Opportunity costs,*" according to Daniel Kahneman, Amos Tversky and Richard Thaler, "*typically receive much less weight than out-of-pocket costs.*"[9] It's conceivable that if the cab driver were to maximize the opportunity to earn money when the weather was bad, he'd easily earn an average of $200 a day.

When investors try to calculate the returns on their portfolios, they often don't bother to use calculators. Instead, they will eyeball the returns or rely on their memories. And when they do, they often make the wrong decisions.

Consider this hypothetical example: Cindy and Ben both make a one-time investment of $10,000 and let it ride for 30 years. Cindy earns 10% on her money, and Ben earns 5%. How much more will Cindy earn over the 30 years than Ben does?

A. 5% more

B. Twice as much more

C. 30% more

D. Four times more

Many people quickly assume that Cindy's investment will earn twice as much as Ben's will. After all, 10% is twice as much as 5%. This error is particularly eye-opening because, when you look at the actual numbers, you can see that the answer is D—Cindy would actually earn over four times as much as Ben in 30 years (see Figure 8.1).

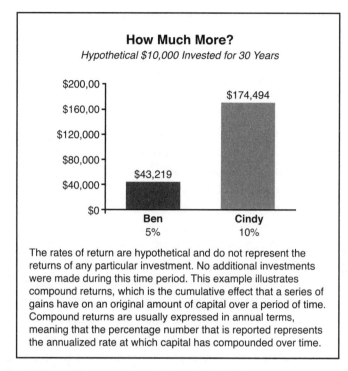

**How Much More?**

*Hypothetical $10,000 Invested for 30 Years*

The rates of return are hypothetical and do not represent the returns of any particular investment. No additional investments were made during this time period. This example illustrates compound returns, which is the cumulative effect that a series of gains have on an original amount of capital over a period of time. Compound returns are usually expressed in annual terms, meaning that the percentage number that is reported represents the annualized rate at which capital has compounded over time.

**Figure 8.1 What difference does 5% really make?**

## *The Most Numbing Number of All*

We hear a lot about "our number" for retirement, the amount we need to comfortably retire. Truth is that nobody really knows what that number is. There are too many variables and complexities. As Americans live longer, the financial services industry is switching the emphasis of its messaging from accumulating assets to making existing assets last. Converting assets into income that can last for the rest of our lives is a complex process and involves a long list of issues, including longevity, inflation, liquidity, Social Security benefits, guarantees, market performance possibilities, and healthcare. A typical question is, *"How much can I spend without running out of money?"*

Unfortunately, the most common method among Boomers for determining the amount of money needed for retirement is…"guessing." Few have tried to systematically figure out how much money they will need to accumulate by the time they retire. And not one person in our focus groups had a good sense of how much money they will need to have by the time they retire.

There are any number of ways that advisers calculate retirement income, including the Monte Carlo Simulation, which is a financial planning tool that is supposed to account for hundreds of thousands of potential market scenarios, guided by assumptions about inflation, volatility, and other parameters.[10] But no formula can help you predict the future, including the Monte Carlo Simulation. There is no set percentage of a retirement nest egg that is proper if you don't want to outlive your money. Every person's situation (health, expenses, and desires) is different, but generally a 4% annual withdrawal is considered a reasonable amount. Although a 4% withdrawal rate doesn't provide any guarantees, it is clear that rates above that level can significantly increase the risk of running out of money. Sound income planning is needed to achieve an income base that can cover essential expenses while providing access to other liquid assets to cover discretionary spending. According to a 2009 consumer study, after the Meltdown of 2008, Americans are now placing a premium on preserving principal, and 80% of those surveyed report they are now more concerned with guarantees and stability than they are with returns as they head toward retirement.[11]

# Improve Your Retirementology IQ

When it comes to your financial plans for retirement, especially in a post-meltdown world, complexity is the order of the day. No longer can you simply find an investment that has a good track record, stuff your money in there, and call it a solid investment. On top of that, an equity investment worth a lot of money does not necessarily represent your retirement nest egg. Chances are that your house is worth more than it was when you bought it, in spite of the meltdown, and you may have other assets. To be ready to retire, however, you're going to have to look at these assets in another way.

Selling assets results in tax penalties, many of which can be avoided. A desire to leave something to your family or to a charity can be compromised by tax considerations as well. A major key to an enjoyable retirement is consistent income that pays for the things that are important to you. First step: Develop an income strategy.

### *Develop an Income Strategy*

As Yogi Berra said, *"When you come to the fork in the road, take it."* And as you rethink the complexity of retirement, you may be asking yourself, *"I've come to the fork in the road. I've taken it. Where do I go from here?"* Before you take a step in any direction, develop an income strategy. The questionnaire in Figure 8.2 identifies key areas that are specific to your needs and can help you anticipate and calculate retirement expenses.

| Anticipated Retirement Expenses | | | |
|---|---|---|---|
| **Write your estimated monthly expenses in the Necessary or Discretionary Column** | | **Necessary** | **Discretionary** |
| Housing | Mortgage/Rent/Fees | $ | $ |
| | Property Taxes and Insurance | | |
| | Utilities | | |
| | Household Improvement | | |
| | Household Maintenance | | |
| Food | At Home | | |
| | Dining Out | | |
| Transportation | Vehicle Purchases/Payments | | |
| | Auto Insurance and Taxes | | |
| | Fuel and Maintenance | | |
| Healthcare | Health Insurance | | |
| | Medicare/Medigap | | |
| | Co-pays/Uncovered Medical Services | | |
| | Drugs and Medical Supplies | | |
| Personal Insurance | Life/Other | | |
| | Long-Term Care | | |
| Personal Care | Clothing | | |
| | Products and Services | | |
| | Entertainment & Hobbies | | |
| | Education | | |
| | Income Taxes | | |
| | Gifts/Charitable Contributions | | |
| | Other | | |
| | | | |
| | | | |
| | Subtotal | $ | $ |
| | Total Necessary & Discretionary Monthly Expenses | | $ |
| | | | X            12 |
| | Total Projected Annual Expenses | | $ |

**Figure 8.2a   Determining your retirement expenses.**

| Existing and Potential Sources of Income | | | | | |
|---|---|---|---|---|---|
| Retirement Savings and Investments | Where Assets Are Held (name of institution) | Short-Term Securities (i.e, cash/money markets) | Bonds (i.e, both bonds and bond funds | Stocks (i.e., both stocks and stock funds) | Total Assets |
| Employer-Sponsored Retirement Plans (401(k)s, 403 (b)s, SEPs, etc.) | | $ | $ | $ | $ |
| IRAs (Traditional, Roth, Rollover) | | | | | |
| Taxable Mutual Funds and Individual Securities | | | | | |
| Savings Accounts, Checking Accounts, and CDs | | | | | |
| Annuities and Life Insurance | | | | | |
| Pension Plans | | | | | |
| Social Security | | | | | |
| Other _____ | | | | | |
| Tangible Assets | | | | | |
| Real Estate | | | | | |
| Other_____ | | | | | |
| Total Retirement Savings/Investments and Tangible Assets | | | | | $ |
| Income Source | Description of Additional Sources of Income (including timeframes) | | | | Monthly Income |
| Social Security, Pension, Part-Time Work, and Rental Income | | | | | $ |
| Total Monthly Income | | | | | $ |
| | | | | | X          12 |
| Total Projected Annual Income | | | | | $ |

**Figure 8.2b    Determining your sources of income.**

## *Turn Piles into Flows*

Accumulating assets is only the first part of retirement planning. The next, perhaps more important, step is to determine how to convert those assets into income that can last you the rest of your life. So how do you turn a pile of assets into a flow of income? Here are five steps to consider:

1. Identify the challenges you can't control and those you can directly impact.
2. Learn the importance of a reasonable withdrawal rate.
3. Consider creating a plan that provides a lifetime stream of income.
4. Complete the previous profile questionnaire.
5. Work with a holistic adviser to custom design a portfolio suited to your needs.

## *Work with a Holistic Adviser*

No one knows everything, whether the subject is as inconsequential as tiddlywinks or as important as retirement planning. However, a good adviser understands how to help you build a potential solution for retirement, and when you're ready to retire, a holistic adviser understands this more complicated distribution phase. As you approach retirement, questions become very complex: How long will you have to work? How much will you need? How much will you need to fund your retirement? By using an advisory approach that focuses on financial solutions rather than on specific investment products, a holistic adviser can develop sound income strategies to help you through your retirement years.

**YOUR ADVISER CAN HELP YOU WITH THE
EMOTIONS AND COMPLEXITY THAT MUDDY
THE RETIREMENT WATERS.**

# Endnotes

1 Producers Web.com, "Hartford survey finds that few understand retirement benefits," September 10, 2009.

2 Congressional Budget Office, "Federal Budget Deficit Totals $1.4 Trillion in Fiscal Year 2009," November 6, 2009.

3 *The Wall Street Journal,* "Taking the National Debt Seriously," October 11, 2009.

4 Top 40-charts.com, "Disco Fever with the Bee Gees," 2009.

5 Federal Reserve, "Bank Prime Loan Rate Changes: Historical Dates of Changes and Rates," December 2008.

6 Federal Reserve, "Bank Prime Loan Rate Changes: Historical Dates of Changes and Rates," December 2008.

7 Yahoo! Finance, Dow Jones Industrial Average (^DJI): Historical Prices, Dec. 25, 1981–Feb. 5, 1982 and Dec. 25, 1999–Feb. 5, 2000.

8 CNN Money, "Don't Expect another bull market," March 3, 2008.

9 Hersh Shefrin, Beyond Greed and Fear, Oxford University Press, 2000, p. 215.

10 *The Wall Street Journal,* "Odds-On Imperfection: Monte Carlo Simulation," May 2, 2009.

11 MetLife, "The 2009 MetLife Study of the American Dream: Rebooting the American Dream. Shifted. Altered. Not Deleted.," study conducted from January 7–16, 2009.

# 9

## Long-Term Smart®

---

**MONELISTIC:** [mun-ih-*lis*-tik]

The state of being emotionally sound and realistic about monetary decisions. *Shelley's monelistic attitude about her finances allowed her to remove her emotions from her retirement strategy and create a long-term plan with the potential to reach her retirement goals.*

---

After a lifetime of diligently saving, a woman in Tel Aviv, Israel, had accumulated a nest egg of over a $1 million. The grandmother of four didn't believe in investments or banks; in fact, her bank was her mattress, and she had slept on the same mattress for decades. In a surprise gesture, however, the lady's daughter bought her mother a new mattress and threw the old, tattered mattress into the trash. By the time the daughter realized what had happened, it was too late. The garbage truck had already taken the mattress to the dump. A massive search ensued, including beefed-up security hired by the city to keep out thieves and looters attracted by waves of publicity. The million-dollar mattress was never found.[1]

It's now estimated that 1-in-12 families in the United States, 28 million people in all, forego a bank account and simply keep all their money in their mattresses or in a home safe.[2] Sales of home safes have skyrocketed in 2009—up 25% industrywide, according to a survey conducted by the *New York Daily News*.[3] Although it's good news that people are saving more these days—America's savings rate is actually out of the negative for the first time in decades—the bad news is that many are not always saving in a smart way. Many of us are saving with an eye toward the next day and with an aversion to loss, which we've already determined can be detrimental to long-term financial success. We've heard many people say that they wish they would have started financially preparing for retirement earlier in their lives, and I demonstrated the advantage of doing so in the first chapter.

If you have designs on retirement, consider saving and investing with an eye on a decade or two in the future. You need to develop a comfort level as it pertains to risk. You need to overcome the human propensity to procrastinate when it comes to making decisions, especially financial decisions, and start right now so that you have more time to invest and get ready for retirement. Simply put, you need to think long-term smart.

## Investors Behaving Badly

Have you ever heard someone say, *"I would've been a lot better off if I would've waited a few years before I started creating a financial plan for retirement?"* Of course you haven't; it's probably never been said. It's never too early to start. Warren Buffett, the man who battles Bill Gates every year for the title of world's richest man, bought his first stock when he was 11 years old and regrets that even he didn't start investing sooner.[4] Only when you become aware of the behaviors that can hurt your saving, spending, and investing can you identify the effects and consequences of those behaviors and take necessary steps to overcome them. Throughout this book, you've seen some of the most common and destructive behavioral finance biases and how they impact your retirement. Table 9.1 is a quick reference guide of some of the most lethal behaviors and biases we have covered.

**Table 9.1  Destructive Financial Behaviors**

| Behavior | Retirement Consequence | Retirementology Rethink |
|---|---|---|
| Procrastination | Delay building a nest egg and run out of time. | Start preparing right away and protect yourself from yourself by creating and sticking to a financial plan. |
| Overconfidence | One consequence is overrating your preretirement health and underestimating potential post-retirement health issues. | Integrate healthcare costs, such as long-term care, into your overall retirement plan. Out-of-pocket expenses in retirement will most likely keep skyrocketing. |
| Layering | Having layers between you and the money you spend…overspending without awareness with too many credit card swipes and fast retail transactions. | People spend 30% more when they pay with a credit card versus cash. *Try the Retirementology Cash Challenge*: See if you can use cash (and only cash) for one month. It may be inconvenient, but it will open your eyes to overspending. |
| Mental Accounting | Money does not come with labels; people put labels on their money. People assign different purposes for different amounts of money. One consequence is how we view taxes and don't always consider the drain of taxation—and not just income taxes. In short, our system of mental accounting typically leads us to discount the impact of taxes on our lives. | Many people have no idea that they give the government a tax-free loan by over-paying their taxes, because they receive a refund. Calculate your deductions more carefully, and that refund money could be yours all along—to invest or earn interest and add to your retirement accounts. To put the total tax bite into perspective, note that on average, you spend more time working to pay your taxes than you will spend working for food, clothing, and shelter combined. |

*(continues)*

**Table 9.1   Destructive Financial Behaviors (continued)**

| Behavior | Retirement Consequence | Retirementology Rethink |
|---|---|---|
| Myopic Loss Aversion | People hate losing more than they love winning. One consequence is to become overly conservative and lose purchasing power to inflation. | Check your emotions at the door when it comes to investing. Base your decisions on facts and not emotions. |
| Herding | Chasing trends and following the crowd can result in buying high because everyone else is buying the same thing, and selling low because everyone else is selling the same thing. | After the Meltdown of 2008, many people sold securities and put their money into cash. By following the herd, many investors stayed out of stocks from March 2009 through the summer, when the Dow went up about 40%.[5] The trend is not your friend. |
| House Money Effect | Windfalls, winnings, earnings, or "found" money. People are more careless with money that was earned by something other than the sweat of their brow. One consequence is expecting the windfall of home appreciation and home equity to be a retirement nest egg. | Although America's housing crisis may be on the road to recovery, using your home as an ATM or retirement plan is a misguided strategy. |
| Attachment Bias | Holding on to a losing business or stock due to family or emotional attachment can derail your retirement plans. | Keep emotions and family out of your investments. |
| Familiarity Bias | Investors may put a higher percentage of their money in a stock they are familiar with, increasing their risk potential and failing to properly diversify. | Recognize what you *don't* know about investments, especially if you are basing decisions on the *all too familiar*. |

| Behavior | Retirement Consequence | Retirementology Rethink |
|---|---|---|
| Number Numbness | Being overwhelmed by numbers because the numbers are so big, or there are so many, that they're incomprehensible. When looking into how one investment might fare versus another, an investor may just appreciate the significant difference between the two, or fail to appreciate how inflation, taxes, and management fees can turn a 10% return into a 5% return. | This stuff is complicated. Consider working with an adviser who takes a holistic approach to all roads leading to retirement. |

Just knowing what these biases are and how they can affect you in both the short run and the long run can go a long way toward helping manage your money and making the most of your financial plans for retirement.

# Improve Your Retirementology IQ

Whether you know it, when you're thinking long-term smart, you're addressing the four challenges that must be taken into consideration if you're going to enjoy a comfortable retirement. They are *longevity, inflation, volatility,* and your very own *expectations* about retirement. Brought together, these four components bring us an acronym that reads **LIVE**.

**The L in LIVE is for Longevity.** After college football legend Paul "Bear" Bryant coached his final game, a reporter from the *Washington Post* asked the coach what he planned to do in retirement. *"I imagine I'll go straight to the graveyard,"* replied Bear sarcastically in his trademark gravelly southern drawl.[6] He was wrong: His retirement lasted about four weeks before he died of a heart attack.[7] Chances are your retirement will last longer than Bear Bryant's did...a lot longer. The fact is there's a 72% chance today that one member of a 65-year-old couple will reach the age of 85.[8] The good news is that improvements in nutrition, healthcare, and medical technology have led to tremendous breakthroughs in people's health, spiking longevity. The bad news is that global aging may well become as big a threat as global warming. At "Longevity 5," a 2009 international conference on aging, economists, actuaries, bankers, insurance executives, and aging experts concluded, among other things, that longevity risk could bankrupt social insurance programs. David Blake of the Pension Institute at the Cass Business School in London and the chairman of the conference said, *"Economists have not really understood this risk and policyholders are not yet engaged."*

The point is, you are on your own, and you should get *personally* engaged and prepared for a long retirement. Don't assume the government, a company pension, or even your family will bail you out. You certainly don't want to be a healthy, happy 90-year-old who finishes up his morning run by stepping up to the ATM and getting an *Insufficient Funds* notice. How will you ever pay for your vitamin-charged mango smoothie? You want a retirement that's as worry free as it can be from a financial perspective, and that's why it's important to work with your advisor to help make sure you have income as long as you live.

**The I in LIVE is for Inflation.** No matter how long you're around, one thing that will be around with you is inflation. Inflation is the invisible tax that's levied on every purchase as time goes on; it steals the purchasing power of each dollar, which is especially dangerous to a senior citizen living on a fixed income. What may have been a comfortable retirement income ten years ago is today squeezed by inflation because that money doesn't buy nearly as much as it did in the late '90s.

Inflation is like compounding interest in reverse and has averaged 4.6% since 1965,[9] which means that an investment that's yielded 4.6% over the past four decades will leave you with enough money to buy exactly as much as it did then. Inflation makes every dollar worth less than it once was worth; it is to your retirement nest egg what kryptonite is to Superman's ability to leap tall buildings in a single bound.

Think about gasoline prices. In recent years, gas prices have gone up and down. When gas costs more, it isn't any better and it doesn't make you go any farther. It just bites into your budget more than it once did. What's worse is that inflation makes other products that are reliant upon gasoline more expensive. Even low rates of inflation can be highly destructive to a retirement plan, and there's not really anything that an individual investor can do to defeat it. Therefore, it's important to make sure that the reality of inflation is a consideration in any retirement plan—like allocating a portion of your portfolio to help maintain the type of investments that can help you outpace inflation.

**The V in LIVE is for Volatility.** The stock market has historically produced average annual returns significantly higher than most fixed income asset categories. But the problem is that this performance comes with some significant ups and downs, strings of both good and bad years—and who can imagine anything worse than what we just went through? It's important to talk to your adviser about finding ways to plan for your financial future that can help minimize the effects of volatility to help ensure that your money will last as long as you do.

**The E in LIVE is for Expectations.** Finally, most people have expectations about the lifestyle they want to have in retirement. Since the Meltdown of 2008, some of the high-flying expectations of Boomer Nation have been grounded, but have we learned enough lessons from the fall? From an article in *USA Today*, published October 8, 2009, titled *"Being jobless for six months 'grinds on you,'"* a 43-year-old construction worker who had lost his job and his home in recent years and barely had enough food in the refrigerator to feed his family of four, was being interviewed.[10] As he talked to the reporter, it was observed that his 13-year-old daughter was curled up on the couch *texting* a friend on her cell phone. Now it is tragic that so many workers have been devastated by record unemployment, but a visual of an empty fridge juxtaposed against the cell phone-equipped tween on the couch could be the movie poster for America's nightmare on Main Street. Clearly, the lessons to be learned from 2008's economic spiral will be harder for some than others. Shaping expectations for retirement should start with reality, not a dream. And a well-constructed retirement plan is a lifelong commitment.

# The American Dream: Rethought

In the span of a single generation, the American nightmare that was the Great Depression turned into the American Dream. It was an amazing cultural transformation. One generation experienced widespread unemployment, soup lines, and severe doubts about the future of America and its economic system. The next generation grew up in single-family houses that their parents were in the process of owning; they ate three square meals a day and went to sock hops on Saturday nights. An entire generation learned that things were always getting better. *"New and improved"* became a part of the American lexicon as every year brought something new for every product, and the old products went hurtling toward obsolescence.

With the notable exception of the '70s, the American economy has grown almost continually since the end of World War II. Products and services became more effective, and the lives of Americans from coast to coast were improved with each new invention, patent, and upgrade. Houses increased in size and square footage as features that were once considered luxuries, such as granite countertops, Jacuzzi tubs, and media rooms, became default items for many homebuilders. Car buyers were basing their decisions on how many cup holders a certain vehicle had, and people were shelling out hundreds of dollars to put their *tweens* in the front rows of the latest boy band concerts. Money was easy, credit was easier, and life was good. Or so we thought.

This same underprepared, overspent, and poorly behaved generation is hurtling toward retirement—kicking, screaming, denying, and determined to reinvent reality. Yes, even before the Meltdown of 2008, Boomers were unprepared for retirement. *We all get it.* But the good news is that 81% of Boomers say the meltdown will cause a major shift in their financial behavior in how they manage their investments and behave with their money.[11] The question is, *"What will that effect be?"* And the more important question is, *"What will you do next?"*

Now that you have a better understanding of the way your mind works with your money, you may be better prepared to apply that insight to the way you approach retirement planning. Here are ten top-of-mind takeaways for improving your Retirementology IQ.

### Top Ten Lessons for Retirementology

1. Prudent financial behavior means being aware of the psychological financial traps.

2. We are in the midst of the worst financial crisis most Americans have ever seen—and it may get worse.

3. Unrealistic lifestyle expectations make a happy retirement impossible.

4. Retirement isn't a singular event—spending in your 20s, 30s, and 70s has an impact on your retirement. Further, retirement isn't isolated—what you spend on a vacation or a car may impact your retirement later.

5. Retirement isn't a zone; it's a continuum—one you need to start thinking about much sooner than five years out.

6. Your home is not a retirement account.

7. Financial support decisions for extended families will move front and center and will have an impact on your retirement.

8. Although historically it has always been part of the mix, taxation is emerging as the single largest financial challenge for the affluent.[12]

9. Healthcare policy and expense will have the potential to sabotage your retirement plan.

10. Your adviser can help you with the emotions and complexity that muddy the retirement waters.

Planning for retirement is a complicated, lifelong commitment; there are no shortcuts or one-size-fits-all solutions. A once-in-a-generation financial meltdown does have a dramatic way of magnifying the need and urgency for a new way of thinking, so approach retirement as a process rather than a vision. This will better prepare you to meet the challenges that no previous generation has had to face before. You can take the first step in *Retirementology* by making a few small changes in your perspective, behavior, and habits in earning, spending, saving, borrowing, and investing. Over time, these small changes may make a big difference in determining how you define retirement and spend your Golden Years.

### LIVE LONG-TERM SMART.

# Endnotes

1 CNN.com, "Tel Aviv search for mattress containing $1M life savings," June 10, 2009.

2 Red Orbit, "Many in U.S. Don't Have Bank Accounts," June 23, 2007.

3 *New York Daily News*, "Stashing the cash at home: Buying a safe to keep your money safe," February 9, 2009.

4 Warren Buffett.com, "Warren Buffett Biography," 2009.

5 *The New York Times*, "Dow, First Time in a Year, Breaks Through 10,000," October 15, 2009.

6 *The Victoria Advocate*, "Heart Attack Claims Coaching Legend," January 25, 1983.

7 *The Victoria Advocate*, "Heart Attack Claims Coaching Legend," January 25, 1983.

8 Employee Benefit Research Institute, July 2005; Society of Actuaries, 2000 Mortality Table.

9 InflationData.com, "Historical US Inflation Rate 1914–Present," 2009.

10 *USA Today*, "Being jobless for 6 months or more 'grinds on you,'" October 7, 2009.

11 MetLife, "The 2009 MetLife Study of the American Dream," study conducted January 7–16, 2009.

12 *Investment Advisor*, "Even Affluent Clients Feel the Chill," October 1, 2008.

# Reterminology _____

## The New Language of Retirement

**401(hey!):** [fohr-oh-wuhn-hey]
The shocked response heard 'round America when people received their 1st quarter 2009 401(k) statements. *Audrey did a 401(hey!) when she opened her mail last week.*

**BINGEIFIED:** [*binj*-ih-fahyd]
The act of justifying a big-ticket purchase because one has been previously frugal. *Shannon had avoided Starbucks for an entire month, so she felt her trip to Maui was bingeified.*

**CLUB FAMWICH:** [kluhb *fam*-wich]
A situation in which multiple generations of a family live in the same house. *The Paulsens have taken on their aging parents, and two of their adult kids have moved back in—it's the ultimate club famwich.*

**DAMNESIA:** [dam-*nee*-zhuh]
Prepurchase state of forgetting how badly it will feel when the damn credit card bill arrives. *James later blamed the damnesia when he plopped his Amex down for the full-carbon mountain bike.*

**EQUIMORTIS:** [ek-wi-*mawr*-tis]
Dangerous condition that can occur from counting on one's home appreciation for retirement money. *Only after the tenth foreclosure hit Colleen and Larry's neighborhood did they realize that they were in a later stage of equimortis.*

**EXTEND and PRETEND:** [ik-*stend* and pri-*tend*]
The mistaken belief and expectation that one can make up for procrastination and colossal underpreparing by merely postponing one's
retirement date by a handful of years. *Patty's extend and pretend
post-meltdown strategy may make her feel better but is unlikely to be
effective.*

**FINANCIA NERVOSA:** [fi-*nans*-see-uh nurv-*ohz*-ah]
An overwhelming fear of the market that causes one to put finances
in limbo. *After the meltdown, Sara's financia nervosa kicked in, and
she stashed all her money into her savings account.*

**FINERTIA:** [*fi*-nur-*shuh*]
Paralysis by analysis brought on by trying to comprehend contradict-
ing and confusing financial information. *After reading the finance
magazines, talking to his friends, and watching an investment show,
Sam was overcome with finertia and now doesn't know what to do
with his money.*

**GOLDEN COWBOY:** [*gohl*-duhn *kou*-boi]
One who fears a collapsing government and economy and begins
hoarding gold and guns. *Dexter was already nervous that the Dow
dipped below 6,700, but when the Chrysler preferred shareholders
got hosed, he went totally golden cowboy.*

**HELLTHCARE:** [*helth*–kair]
*Hell*thcare is what Medicare has become for many. *Trying to manage
the paperwork and red tape that followed her surgery was sheer
hellthcare for Gina.*

**HOME ALONE** [hohm uh-**lohn**]
The state of a house having no investment value—current or likely in
the near future—having value only as a place to sleep. *Given that an
identical model to the Sneider's sold for about $100,000 less than
what they paid for their half-million dollar home, they knew they
were home alone.*

**HOMEOPATHIC:** [hoh-mee-uh-*path*-ik]
An abnormal and expensive psychological devotion or attachment to one's home. *When George finished the exterior deck in marble, we knew he was homeopathic.*

**HOUSEPITAL:** [*hous*-pi-tl]
What one's home becomes when caring for a family member long term due to the inability to pay a provider. *Many people caring for their elderly parents have turned their homes into housepitals.*

**IFONLIES:** [if-*ohn*-lees]
The large portion of Americans who now wish they had put money away instead of spending. *After years of mismanaging their money, America's many ifonlies have switched to a frugal lifestyle.*

**INSTAPIDITY:** [in-stuh-*pid*-i-tee]
The compulsion of making big purchases immediately instead of saving to buy them later. *The instapidity of consumers these days could just cost them their retirement.*

**KINPHOBIA:** [kin-*foh*-bee-uh]
Fear of having to dig into retirement money to financially help one's family—that is, adult children, siblings, in-laws, or aging parents. *When Barry's wife explained to him that her unemployed mother was cashing in her IRA to buy a time share, his kinphobia kicked in.*

**LAYER CAKING:** [*ley*-er keyk-ing]
Putting multiple psychological layers of distance between yourself and your money by using money proxies. *Herb was layer caking like crazy when he gave the bartender his room number and bought round after round for the group last night.*

**LOAN RANGER:** [lohn *reyn*-jer]
One who uses his home's equity like an ATM, while also expecting to fund retirement with it down the road. *Before the housing bust, loan ranger Jim could be heard yelling "hi-ho-silver" from the rooftop of his beautiful home, expecting to ride its double-digit appreciation into the sunset of retirement.*

**MONELERIOUS:** [mun-ih-*lair*-ee-*uhs*]
The state of being wildly incorrect in one's thinking about any given money matter. *Investors were monelerious before the meltdown— expecting double-digit returns on their portfolios and home values to double in the next five years.*

**MONELISTIC:** [mun-ih-*lis*-tik]
The state of being emotionally sound and realistic about monetary decisions. *Shelley's monelistic attitude about her finances allowed her to remove her emotions from her retirement strategy and create a long-term plan with the potential to reach her retirement goals.*

**NEURO SQUABBLE:** [noo-roh *skwob*-uhl]
The classic power struggle between one's left brain (reason) and one's right brain (emotion). *Gary's neuro squabble lasted for two days when deciding whether to invest his bonus in the stock market or use it to purchase a flat-screen TV. Unfortunately for his retirement account, his right brain won out.*

**NUMBERTOSE:** [nuhm-ber-tohs]
The state of being overwhelmed by the numbers and equations one must contemplate to plan their financial future. *After spend- ing the evening determining how much money he and his wife would need for a comfortable retirement, Mark was completely numbertose.*

**OHNOSIS:** [oh-*noh*-sis]
Realizing that you really should have started planning for retirement years ago. *After John completed the online retirement calculator, he was struck with a severe case of ohnosis.*

**PLASTIC SURGERY:** [*plas*-tik *sur-juh-ree*]
Any kind of major change in lifestyle that's designed to eliminate credit card dependence or debt. *Rita and Bob are undergoing plastic surgery to get their finances in line.*

**PROBATIOUS:** [proh-*bey*-shuhs]
Incivility of a family member squabbling over an inheritance. *Mar- garet's oldest daughter was simply probatious after the funeral.*

**RETIREMENTOLOGY:** [ri-*tahy*<sup>uh</sup>r-muhnt-*ol*-uh-jee]
A new way of thinking about retirement planning that considers both psychology and finance against a backdrop of the worst economic crisis since the Great Depression.

**RETIREWENT:** [ri-*tahy*<sup>uh</sup>r-went]
What happened to the retirement hopes and dreams of Americans after the meltdown. *Roger and Dee both had to take on second jobs thanks to retirewent.*

**SHADOW MILLIONAIRE:** [shad-oh mil-*yuh*-*nair*]
Person fortunate enough to still receive a guaranteed pension for life. *No one would have guessed that retired schoolteacher, Miss Miller, was indeed a shadow millionaire.*

**SNEAKERS:** [snee-kerz]
The small but numerous and vague tax charges on phone bills, hotel bills, utility bills, and so on. *Amanda was outraged by all the little sneakers that added up to over $14 on her phone bill.*

**TAX RACKET:** [taks *rak*-it]
The government's continual raising of taxes. *In recent years, the tax racket had taken its toll on Jim's monthly expenses.*

**TAXADERMY:** [*tak*-sah-dur-mee]
The painful process of being taxed to death by the government. *George and his wife packed up and moved from California to Texas to avoid taxadermy.*

**VIGORISTIC:** [vig-er-*is*-tik]
Overconfidence in one's ability to remain healthy, often resulting in a lack of critical financial healthcare planning. *He was vigoristic about not needing long-term care insurance.*

**ZONED OUT:** [zohnd out]
Irrationally believing that one can tune out retirement-related decisions because he is not yet "in the zone." *Because he did not plan on retiring for 15 more years, Andy zoned out on his retirement planning.*

**ZOOMERS:** [zoo-merz]
Over-caffeinated, over-stimulated Boomers spending $5–$20 a day on brown liquid. *That zoomer was so hyped up on his macchiato with an extra shot that he couldn't sit still during the board meeting.*

# INDEX